Change and conflict

Britain, Ireland and Europe
from the late 16th to the early 18th centuries

CAMBRIDGE
UNIVERSITY PRESS

For Rose and David

Published by the Press Syndicate of the University of Cambridge
The Pitt Building, Trumpington Street, Cambridge CB2 1RP
40 West 20th Street, New York, NY 10011-4211, USA
10 Stamford Road, Oakleigh, Melbourne 3166, Australia
© Cambridge University Press 1994

First published 1994

Printed in Great Britain by the University Press, Cambridge

A catalogue record for this book is available from the British Library

Library of Congress cataloguing in publication data applied for

ISBN 0 521 46603 2 paperback

Picture research by Callie Kendall

Illustrations by Nick Asher, Martin Sanders, Sue Shields

Notice to teachers
Many of the sources used in this textbook have been adapted or abridged from the original.

Front cover illustrations: 'The Battle of the Boyne' by Jan Wyck, 1690, courtesy of the Director, National Army Museum, London. Ptolemy, 'Geographiae Universae', 1597.

Acknowledgements
Every effort has been made to reach copyright holders; the publisher would be glad to hear from anyone whose rights they have unwittingly infringed.
6t, Genoese world map, by permission of the Syndics of Cambridge University Library; 6b, Mappe Monde c. 1730, by permission of the Syndics of Cambridge University Library; 7t, Istituto e Museo di Storia della Scienza di Firenze/photo by Franca Principe; 8, The Master and Fellows of Magdalene College, Cambridge; 9r, 51b, 68, British Library, London; 9l, Bibliothèque Nationale; 13t, Mary Evans Picture Library (photo Charnet)/Explorer; 13b, Statens Konstmuseer, Stockholm; 16-17(background), from Theatrum Orbis Terrarum, 1584, by permission of the Syndics of Cambridge University Library; 16, 18, 65, Mary Evans Picture Library; 19, The Granger Collection; 22, 23t, National Maritime Museum, Greenwich; 23b, 24r, 25, 45, 49, 54,62, by courtesy of the National Portrait Gallery, London; 24l, Private Collection/ Bridgeman Art Library, London; 30t, from J. Derricke, The Image of Ireland, 1581, by permission of the Syndics of Cambridge University Library; 30bl, 40t, courtesy of The Educational Company of Ireland; 30r-31, National Museum of Ireland; 31b, Tate Gallery, London; 32, The Board of Trustees of the Royal Armouries; 33, 41, National Library of Ireland; 38, courtesy of Thomas Ryan, RHA; 39, 40b, Lambeth Palace Library; 48l, 51tr, Fotomas Index; 51tl, by permission of the Syndics of Cambridge University Library; 53, Carmel Gallagher; 60, Museum of London/Bridgeman Art Library, London; 66, 69, Ulster Museum, Belfast; 71, courtesy of the Director, National Army Museum, London; 74, National Gallery of Ireland; 76, Office of Public Works/photo courtesy of Blackstaff Press; 77t, Leeds City Art Galleries; 77b, Illustrated London News Picture Library; 78, Towneley Hall Art Gallery & Museum, Burnley/Bridgeman Art Library, London; 79, Christopher Hill Photographic

The publisher would like to thank the following for their contributions: Carmel Gallagher, Tony McAleavy and Sheela Speers.

CONTENTS

Introduction:
A changing world 1400–1700

Section 1:
The causes of European rivalries from the 16th to the early 18th centuries

Section 2:
The experience of colonisation and plantation

Section 3:
The causes and consequences of political and religious conflicts in the British Isles 1630–1655

Section 4:
The causes and consequences of the Williamite Wars

Introduction

A changing world 1400–1700

People living in Europe in the 15th and 16th centuries were living in a time of great change. From your study of the Normans you will know that their period in history is called the Middle Ages or Medieval Times. In this book we will be studying the period of time in history which followed the Middle Ages and is called Early Modern Times. Historians use that name because many of the changes that took place at that time helped to shape our modern world.

What were these changes and what effects did they have?

Europe was ruled by kings and princes.

The Catholic Church was the main Christian Church. The Reformation introduced the Protestant Churches.

Farming was very important. There were few merchants. Most people lived in the countryside or small villages.

Catholic teaching influenced all learning and knowledge. Books were hand-written in Latin. The known world was small. Few people explored new regions of the Earth.

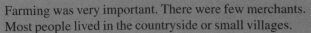

1200	1300	1400

Medieval Times

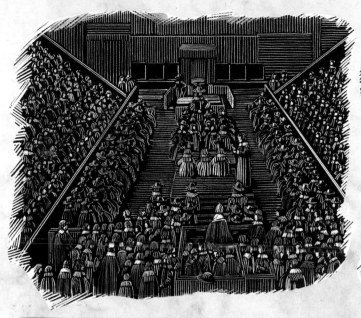

Parliaments became more important in making laws and ruling in some countries.

The Church had great influence over rulers and people. Europe was divided by religion and this led to wars of religion.

Merchants became more powerful, commerce and trade more widespread. Cities and towns became more important.

Increasing knowledge of science and nature challenged old ideas. Many books were printed in different languages. New inventions and new types of ship led to voyages of exploration, the setting up of colonies and world trade.

1500　　　　　　　　**1600**　　　　　　　　**1700**

Early Modern Times

Exploring the world

Before 1500, people in Britain and Europe knew very little about other parts of the world. Over the next 200 years, improvements in ships and navigation made it possible for European sailors to travel long distances and explore new lands. The countries they discovered often had rich natural resources like gold and silver mines in America. Many places in the East produced goods such as expensive silks and new spices which became the basis of wealth and trade for the European countries.

Source A

This is a map of the 'known' world as people believed it to be in 1457.

● *Can you identify Ireland?*

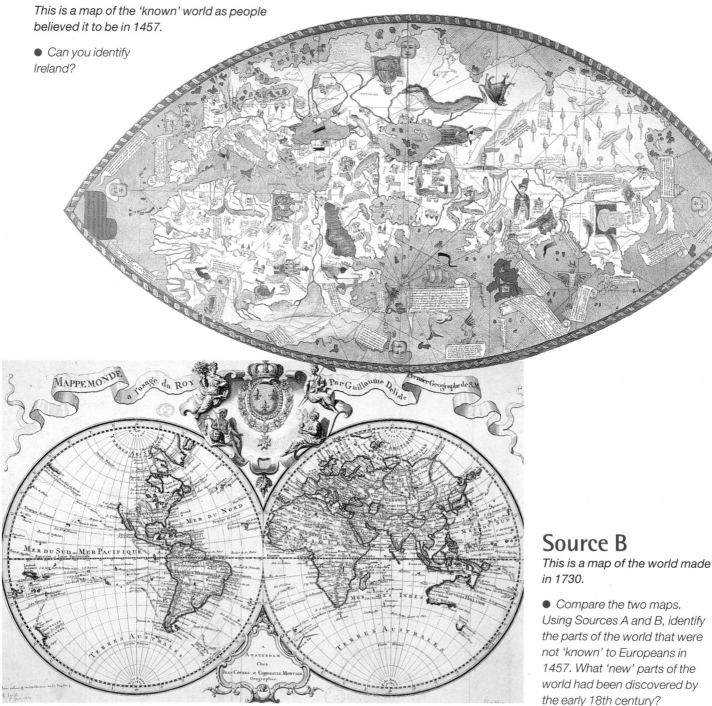

Source B

This is a map of the world made in 1730.

● *Compare the two maps. Using Sources A and B, identify the parts of the world that were not 'known' to Europeans in 1457. What 'new' parts of the world had been discovered by the early 18th century?*

Exploring the universe

In the 16th and 17th centuries, people became more and more interested in explaining the world around them. At the beginning of this period, people believed that God or the Devil caused mysterious happenings. By the end of the 17th century, discoveries in medicine, mathematics, physics, astronomy and many other subjects had changed people's attitudes. Many of these new discoveries challenged the teachings of the Church.

● After 1520 people began to challenge the Catholic Church, which had not been willing to think about new ideas about the world.

● Technical improvements between 1580 and 1620 meant that better instruments such as microscopes and telescopes were invented.

● Before 1500 people believed that the Earth was fixed at the centre of the universe and that the Sun and the other planets circled around it. The Church taught that God created the Earth as the centre of the universe.

● In 1543 a Polish scholar called Copernicus wrote a book which suggested that the Sun, not the Earth, was the centre of the universe.

● In the 1620s an Italian named Galileo used a telescope to prove that Copernicus's ideas were correct. Galileo's works were banned by the Catholic Church.

● Before 1600 people put forward ideas without trying to test or prove them. Francis Bacon, writing at the beginning of the 17th century, said that scientists should base their ideas on experiment and observation.

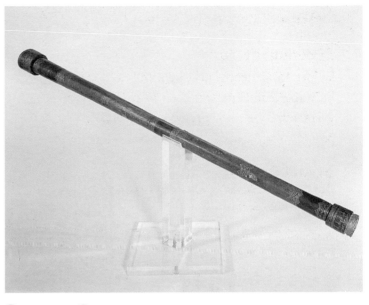

Source C

Telescopes like these, which had several lenses, were developed from about 1600. They made it possible for people to learn more about the universe.

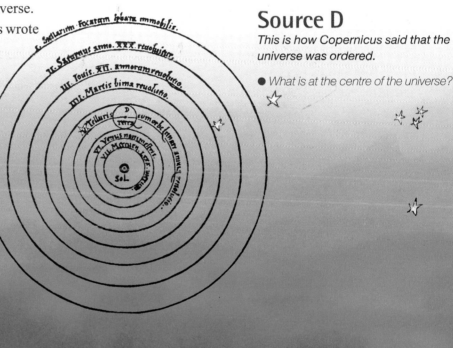

Source D

This is how Copernicus said that the universe was ordered.

● *What is at the centre of the universe?*

PROSPECTUS INTRA CAMERAM STELLATAM.

Scientists and inventors

In the 16th and 17th centuries, Isaac Newton developed scientific theories which completely changed our understanding of the forces which control the universe and his ideas still remain relevant today. Using mathematics, he showed that planets in the solar system are held together by a force called gravity. He tried to explain the way the planets move around the Sun.

According to a popular story, Newton's ideas about gravity were prompted when an apple fell on his head while he was sitting under a tree. Why do things like apples fall to earth when other things like the moon do not? Newton showed that the planets are kept in place by two forces: their own speed and the gravitational pull of the Sun upon them.

● *The story about Newton and the apple is not true. Why do you think people still tell it?*

When Newton died he was succeeded as president of the Royal Society by Sir Hans Sloane, a physician who treated Queen Anne and George II. Hans Sloane was born in 1660 in Killyleagh, County Down. He played an important part in introducing immunisation against smallpox. When he died his collection of specimens and books formed the basis of what is now the British Museum. Hans Sloane had been taught by Robert Boyle who is regarded as the father of modern chemistry. Boyle was a physicist and chemist who was born in Munster in 1627. In 1661 he explained how the pressure and volume of gases are related to each other. This important discovery is called Boyle's Law.

Spreading new ideas

Before the invention of the printing press, every book had to be copied by hand, often by monks in monasteries. Books were, therefore, rare and expensive. A goldsmith called Gutenberg set up the first European printing press in Germany in 1450. William Caxton set up the first English printing press in Westminster in 1476. Fifty years after the invention of printing there were probably about 20 million books in Europe.

By 1600, 150 years after the invention of printing, there were probably closer to 200 million books. The invention of printing made books much more available and a lot cheaper and so a lot more people had access to them. New ideas and learning therefore spread much more quickly.

Source F – An early printing press

Source G – The first book printed in Ireland, 1571

1 Choose two changes that took place in the Early Modern period and explain why you think they were important.

2 Describe what you think each of the workers might be doing in Source F. What major effects do you think the invention of printing had on the world?

3 Write a short paragraph in your own words explaining why we call this the Early Modern period.

The 16th century

1 The Church

At the beginning of the 16th century most countries in western Europe belonged to the Catholic Church. It was a very wealthy and powerful Church led by the Pope, who lived in Rome. Ordinary people in many countries paid money to the Pope each year to help pay for the upkeep of the Catholic Church and to maintain the Pope's power in Rome and beyond. Latin was the language of the Church. All Church services were in Latin and the Bible was printed in Latin.

2 The Reformation

Some people were critical of the wealth and power of the Catholic Church. They felt that it was very different from the kind of Church which Jesus and his disciples had intended. One of the people who criticised the Church strongly was a German monk called Martin Luther. In 1517 he protested about some Church practices and beliefs which he said should be changed (reformed). He set up his own reformed Protestant Church. Others followed his example by setting up their own reformed Churches. This movement became known as the Reformation.

3 Protestant and Catholic Europe

The Protestant Reformation began in Germany and spread to Scotland, Switzerland and Scandinavia. There were soon two Christian Churches in western Europe – Catholic and Protestant. In the 1530s Henry VIII, King of England, argued with the Pope who would not allow him to divorce his wife. Henry, deciding the Pope had no right to deny him a divorce, made himself head of the Church of England and England broke away from the Church of Rome. France, Spain, Portugal and Ireland remained mainly Catholic although some people in France and the Netherlands (which was ruled by Spain) supported Protestant ideas.

4 Voyages of exploration

In the 15th and 16th centuries there were voyages of exploration from Europe in search of new routes to the East. In 1492, on a voyage financed by Spain, Christopher Columbus sailed westwards searching for a new passage to the Indies. Instead he encountered a previously unknown continent, later to be named the Americas.

5 Colonies in America

In the 16th century, European countries realised that control of America and other 'new' lands was an important way to increase their wealth and power. Countries like Spain and Portugal tried to get control of as much land as possible in the 'New World' by sending settlers to set up 'colonies'. The more land a country acquired, the more powerful it could become. Spain and Portugal, (and later England and France), competed with each other to gain control of large areas of America. Spain acquired by far the most land and the most colonies.

6 Elizabeth and Philip

Elizabeth I was Queen of England from 1558 until 1603. Philip II was King of Spain from 1556 until 1598. Philip had been married to Elizabeth's half-sister, Queen Mary, who was a Catholic. When Elizabeth became Queen after Mary died, Philip asked her to marry him but she refused. After this Elizabeth and Philip became great enemies. Philip believed it was his role to defend the Catholic faith; Elizabeth felt it was her role to defend the Protestant faith.

1

The Reformation

In 1500 most Europeans belonged to the Catholic Church and accepted the Pope as its head.
By the end of the 16th century many Christians no longer belonged to the Catholic
Church and no longer recognised the Pope as their leader.

Why did the Reformation happen?

The Catholic Church had become very rich and powerful by 1500 but many people believed that the Church was not following the teaching of Jesus and his early disciples. Nevertheless, in many countries like England the Church was popular and had a strong following.

The Reformation was caused not so much because ordinary people wanted the Church to be reformed, but because rulers like King Henry VIII wanted to be free from the power which the Church and the Pope had over him and his subjects.

Criticisms of the Church

▶ **The Pope**
Popes often behaved more like powerful kings than religious leaders. Some plotted to become rich and did not care about teaching religion or controlling their priests and bishops. Rulers disliked having to pay large sums of money to the Pope in Rome.

▼ **Cardinals and bishops**
Some cardinals and bishops were lazy and greedy for wealth and power. They sold Church jobs for money and were often absent from their dioceses. Some held more than one job in the Church and many even gave Church posts to their relatives.

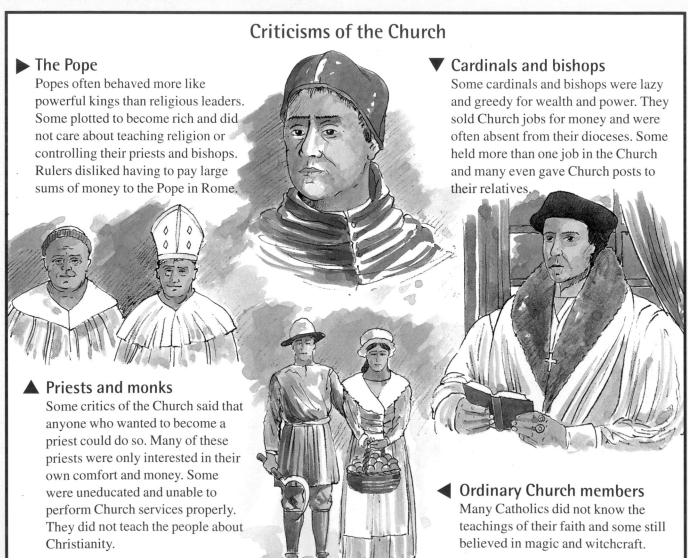

▲ **Priests and monks**
Some critics of the Church said that anyone who wanted to become a priest could do so. Many of these priests were only interested in their own comfort and money. Some were uneducated and unable to perform Church services properly. They did not teach the people about Christianity.

◀ **Ordinary Church members**
Many Catholics did not know the teachings of their faith and some still believed in magic and witchcraft.

Challenging the Church

Many of the abuses within the Church had been going on for some time but in the late 15th century new ideas were beginning to challenge the control of the Church. The development of printing helped to spread new ideas to many more people.

Source A

This is an extract from a late 15th-century account of how Rodrigo Borgia, a Spanish cardinal, was elected Pope Alexander VI:

> Borgia (later elected Pope Alexander VI) openly bribed many of the cardinals, some with money and some with promises of profitable jobs.
> The cardinals, with no thought for what the gospel says, were not ashamed to take bribes.

Source B

This complaint was written by a German monk in 1493 about other monks in his monastery:

> All is confusion. If we look at the holy service, they perform it in such a confused way their words make no sense. They understand nothing at all of what they sing. The Bible is never seen in their hands.

Source C – Martin Luther

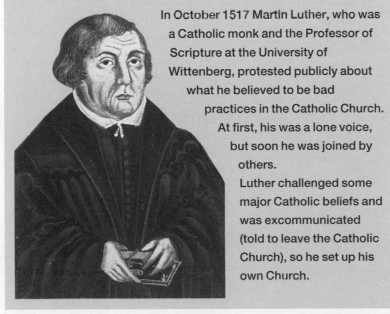

In October 1517 Martin Luther, who was a Catholic monk and the Professor of Scripture at the University of Wittenberg, protested publicly about what he believed to be bad practices in the Catholic Church. At first, his was a lone voice, but soon he was joined by others.

Luther challenged some major Catholic beliefs and was excommunicated (told to leave the Catholic Church), so he set up his own Church.

Source D – John Calvin

John Calvin was the most influential reformer apart from Luther. He was a French lawyer and priest who lived in Switzerland. His ideas spread through many countries in western Europe but they were based on harsh discipline and were criticised by other Christians. This vicious caricature by a Catholic artist shows Calvin's face as being made up of various pieces of meat and fish.

The new Churches

Critics of Catholic beliefs and practices, such as Calvin and Zwingli, followed Luther's example by setting up their own Churches. This movement is known as the Reformation. They were called Protestants because they protested that, for example, they wanted the Bible and Church services to be written in the language of the people, not Latin. In time they achieved many of their aims.

- In 1526 the first Bible was printed in English.
- In 1549 the Book of Common Prayer was printed in English.
- In 1568 the Book of Common Order was printed in Gaelic for Scottish and Irish Protestants.
- In 1571 the first book printed in Ireland was a Protestant Catechism printed in Gaelic.

What were the effects of the Reformation?

Many rulers in northern Europe had been jealous of the wealth and power of the Catholic Church. The Reformation for them was a way to take over Church land and riches and to make themselves more powerful. Within 50 years, many European countries had become Protestant and the people of these countries were no longer allowed by their rulers to look to the Pope as their religious leader. In England, in the 1530s, King Henry VIII also broke away from the Catholic Church and the Pope of Rome. He declared himself to be head of the Church in England and the official state religion gradually became Protestant. As a result of the Reformation, Europe became divided by religion.

In France and Germany wars of religion broke out. England became a powerful Protestant country in the 16th century under the rule of Queen Elizabeth I. Spain became a powerful Catholic country under the rule of Philip II.

Protestant and Catholic areas of 16th-century Europe

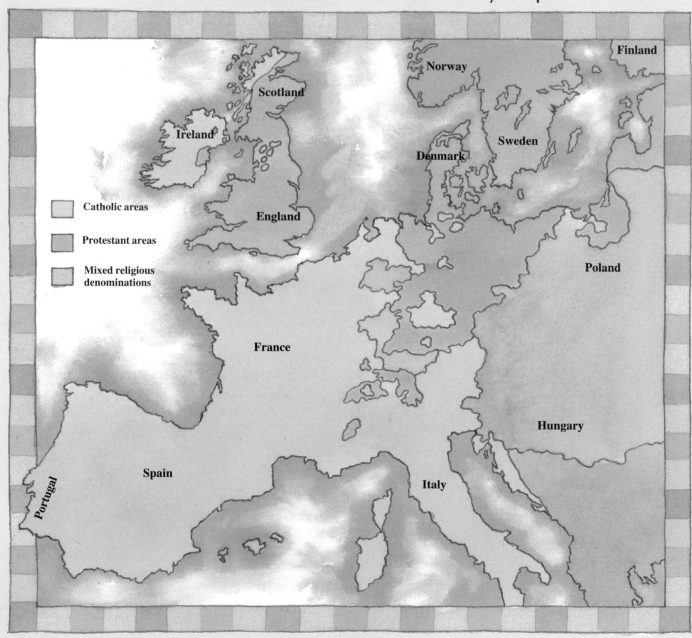

Legend:
- Catholic areas
- Protestant areas
- Mixed religious denominations

causes

The power of the Pope

Abuses in the Church

Martin Luther

New ideas

Printing

Causes ands effects of the Reformation

Wars of religion

A divided Europe

The Counter-Reformation

Spread of Protestant religion

Increased power of monarchs

effects

The Counter-Reformation

As the Reformation spread, the Catholic Church responded by setting up:

● **The Council of Trent**

This was a council of Church leaders which restated Catholic beliefs and removed some of the old abuses.

● **New religious orders**

New religious orders, such as the Jesuits, were founded to improve the standards of religious education and carry out missionary work.

● **The Inquisition**

In Catholic countries like Spain, people suspected of holding Protestant beliefs were questioned by a type of religious court of law, called the Inquisition. Many people were tortured and some were burned at the stake if they refused to change their beliefs. In Protestant countries some Catholics were also persecuted.

The result of this Counter-Reformation was that the Catholic Church remained strong in Spain, France and Italy. The Jesuits established higher standards of Catholic education and sent missionaries to America and Asia to convert the people there to Catholicism.

---

1 Make a list of the criticisms of the Catholic Church before the Reformation.

2 Look at Sources A and B. What were the two authors' views about the Church at that time?

3 Using the map make a list of:
   a Protestant countries;
   b Catholic countries.

4 Copy the map on page 14 to illustrate the religious divisions in Europe in the 16th century. Describe how and why Europe had become divided.

5 Study the location of Ireland on the map and suggest reasons to explain why England might consider Ireland as a possible threat in the 16th century.

6 Write an essay entitled 'The main causes and effects of the Reformation in Europe'. Plan the essay in sections or paragraphs using the diagram on the left to help you.

2

Conflict and colonisation

Christopher Columbus, on an expedition financed by the King of Spain, made his first voyage westwards in search of a new route to the Indies and the East in 1492. He landed on islands off the coast of America which he called the 'Indies'. He did not realise for some time that he had encountered a whole new continent. Spain was the first European country to start setting up colonies on the new continent which they called the Americas.

Why did the discovery of this 'New World' lead to competition and conflict between the major European powers?

Spain and Portugal were the first European countries to undertake voyages of discovery and to benefit from the valuable resources belonging to the lands they 'found'. The other European countries quickly realised the wealth which they could gain from exploration and colonisation and a period of intense rivalry followed as the European powers fought to establish control of these newly discovered lands. At first this competition was peaceful, but after an attack by the Spanish on English ships in a Mexican harbour in 1567, English and Spanish seamen regarded each other as enemies.

Sir Francis Drake

Between 1578 and 1580, Sir Francis Drake and his men became the first Englishmen to sail around the world. It was a raiding voyage and great treasures were brought back, a large portion of which went to the British monarch, Queen Elizabeth I. The activities of sailors like Drake outraged the Spanish King, many of whose vessels were attacked and plundered by British privateers. The Queen, however, was prepared to turn a blind eye to these activities because they brought her so much wealth. Many other British explorers and adventurers visited new lands searching for profitable trading routes and by 1750 Britain was the world's leading trading nation.

Source A
Sir Francis Drake sailed around the world in his ship, the Golden Hind, between 1578 and 1580. This picture of Drake's ship was painted 300 years later.

Rivalry in the New World

Richard Hakluyt was an English clergyman who wrote about the voyages taking place at the end of the 16th century. He encouraged British sailors to explore the world and particularly to find new routes to the East. Like many other people, Hakluyt believed it must be possible to sail to China by navigating north of Russia or Canada. Such a route would mean it was easier to trade with the eastern countries which produced valuable and exotic items such as silk, spices and porcelain. In fact there was no route to the East by sailing north but the voyages that searched for it opened up many other trading routes, for example to the fur- and timber-producing parts of northern Canada.

Source B

The Kings of Spain and Portugal have enlarged their kingdoms, greatly enriched themselves and their subjects, and trebled the size of their navies.

If we follow, there will be huge demands for English cloth, with great benefit for all those who work in the cloth trade. A great number of men, but also children and women who now have no work, will be found employment in making things which can be traded with those who live in new lands.

See what islands and ports you might find by sailing to the north-east, for it would be good that we should have the control over our own trade routes to India and China, and so bring ourselves great riches.

First and foremost…spread the happy news of Jesus to those who know nothing of him. Second…teach them about our knowledge of farming.

Richard Hakluyt, *The Principal Navigations, Voyages and Discoveries of the English Nation, 1589–1600*

● *What were the main reasons given by Hakluyt for undertaking voyages of discovery?*

Source C

This map of the world was drawn in 1584 by Abraham Ortelius.

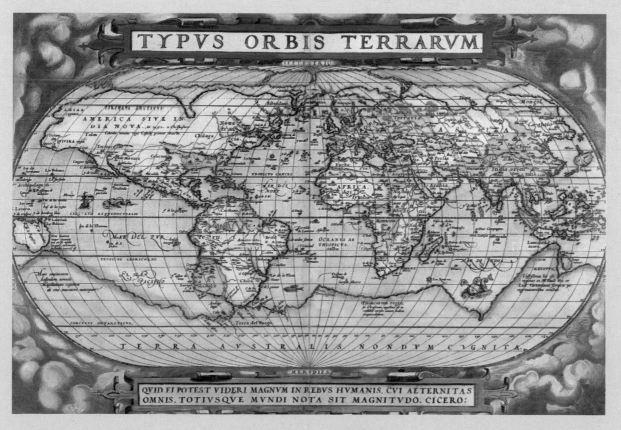

An English colony in the New World

Before any other country had set up one single settlement in the 'New World', as America was called, Spain had set up around 200 different colonies. Great wealth, in the form of gold, silver and other goods, was shipped back to Spain from these Spanish colonies. Britain, like other countries, became jealous of Spanish influence and wealth and began to set up colonies of its own. The following source gives us an insight into what some people felt could be gained from setting up colonies in America.

Source D

These reasons for colonisation were published when the English were setting up the Roanoke colony in North America:

1 The Glory of God by planting religion among those infidels.

2 The possibility of enlarging the dominions of the Queen and therefore of her honour, revenue and power.

3 This realm shall receive wood, oil, wines, hops, salt cheaper than now.

4 The plenty and variety of flesh there may cheaply feed our navies.

5 The passage to and fro is through the main sea so we are not in danger of our enemy's coast.

6 If we have too many young people they may be employed in the mines there, in tilling of the rich soil for grain and in planting of vines there for wine.

7 A great possibility of further discoveries.

8 Sugar canes may be planted as well as they are now in the south of Spain. So we could get it cheaper and not enrich our doubtful friends.

The Chief Reasons for Colonisation, 1585

Source E

A drawing of an Indian chief being captured by English colonists in Virginia, 1608.

Source F

This is an extract from an account written by a visitor to the English colony at Roanoke in North America:

At our first coming to anchor on this shore we saw a great smoke rise in the isle of Roanoke near the place where I left our colony in the year 1587, this put us in good hope that some of the colony were expecting us. And so we passed toward the place where we left them, in 1585 in sundry houses, but we found the houses taken down and the place very strongly enclosed with a high palisade of great trees. We found the grass and sundry rotten trees burning around the place. From there we went along by the waterside toward the point of the creek to see if we could find any of their boats, but we could see no sign of them nor any of the small guns which were left with them on my departure. At our return from the creek some of our sailors meeting us told us that they had found bodies and human remains.

John White, 1590

Although the first English attempt to set up a colony at Roanoke failed, England went on to establish a number of successful colonies in North America: in Maryland in 1634; in Carolina in 1663; and in Georgia in 1733. In time, England controlled most of North America until the end of the American War of Independence in 1783.

Source G – Roanoke deserted

This 19th century engraving shows John White returning to Roanoke Island in 1590 and discovering that the settlement had been abandoned. The word 'Croatoan' was carved on one of the entrance posts and one theory is that the colonists had gone to join the Croatan Indians. However, in spite of various attempts to discover what happened to them, the settlers were never found.

1 Examine Source D. Using your own words, organise reasons for setting up this colony into different groups as in the table below:

Economic reasons	Political reasons	Religious reasons

2 If you were the organiser of this colony, what type of skills would you want your new settlers to have?

3 Look again at Sources D and E. What possible difficulties are hinted at in these sources?

4 List the strengths and weaknesses of the Roanoke colony.

5 Using clues in Source F, describe what you think may have happened to the Roanoke colony. Explain why we cannot be sure of what happened at Roanoke.

6 Write a letter of advice to the organisers of other colonies listing the preparations and precautions they need to take to avoid an experience similar to Roanoke.

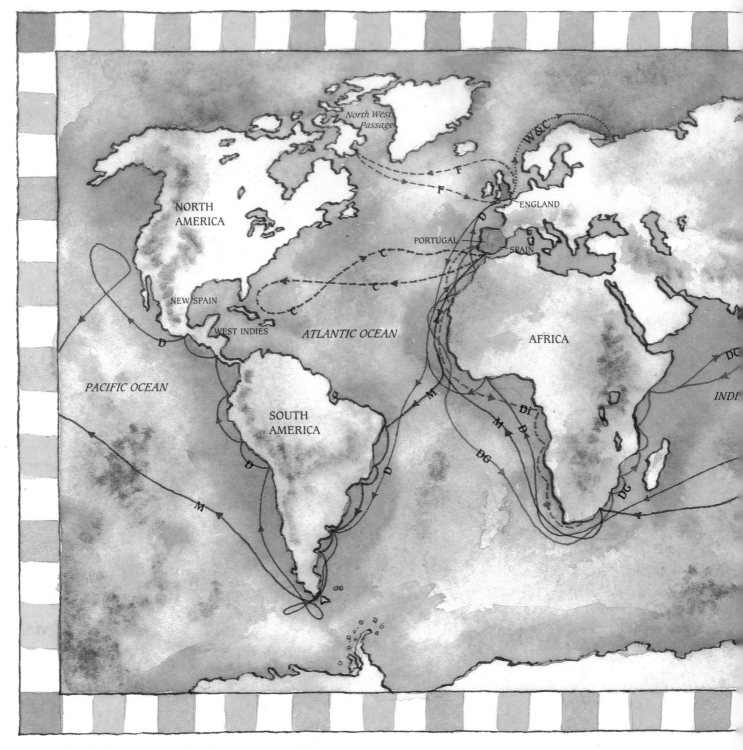

Voyages of discovery in the 15th and 16th centuries

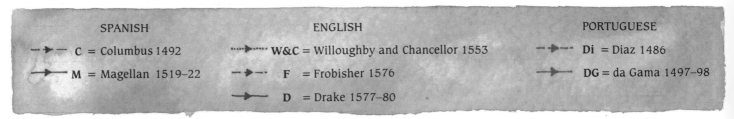

SPANISH	ENGLISH	PORTUGUESE
C = Columbus 1492	W&C = Willoughby and Chancellor 1553	Di = Diaz 1486
M = Magellan 1519–22	F = Frobisher 1576	DG = da Gama 1497–98
	D = Drake 1577–80	

From Britain, ships travelled to
- southern Europe, to trade in fruits
- the Baltic, to trade in fur and timber
- the East Indies, to trade in spices and new, light clothes
- the West Indies, to trade in sugar, tobacco and fruit
- North America, to trade in sugar and timber.

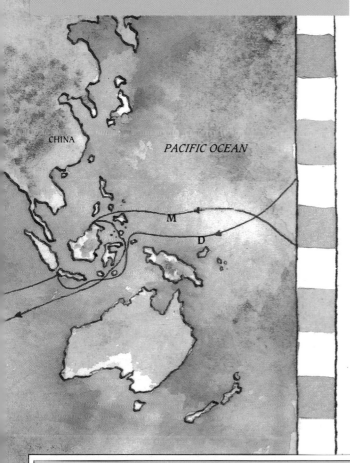

CHINA

PACIFIC OCEAN

M

D

---

1 Compare Source C with the map showing voyages of discovery. Which parts of the world did Ortelius seem to know most about? Which parts did he seem to know least about?

2 Why did British sailors set out on voyages of discovery? Use the evidence in this unit to fill in a table like the one below.

Reason for exploration	Source

Why do you think Richard Hakluyt's work is an important source for a historian?

The results of Britain's exploration and new trade

✶ War

More exploration led to more wars. In Queen Elizabeth I's reign, British seamen fought continually against the Spanish, capturing treasure as they did so. Later, Britain fought wars about trade against the Dutch and the French.

✶ Slavery

British traders became involved with the slave trade. British ships took Africans as slaves to America. There they worked on large plantations, producing sugar and cotton which was then shipped back to Britain. It was a very profitable business for the British, though at huge and terrible human cost.

✶ Wealth

Many people became very wealthy as a result of new trade routes. Bristol became one of the busiest and richest ports in the world.

✶ Settlement

Some people left Britain to settle, and often to control, the lands that had been explored. There were important new settlements in North America, where many Puritans set up new colonies, such as Virginia.

✶ New tastes and goods

Sugar from the West Indies, silks and cottons from the East, and spices from all over the world were brought back to Britain. New crops like potatoes and tobacco were first introduced to Britain from America in the 16th century. Tea and coffee had also been unknown in Britain before 1500.

✶ A powerful nation

The new trade made Britain very powerful. The East India Company, for example, which was founded in 1600, gradually increased its control over large parts of India. The British Crown controlled colonies in North America.

3

Rivalry between England and Spain

In 1588 King Philip II of Spain sent a large Armada of ships filled with soldiers and arms to invade England and remove Queen Elizabeth from the throne.

Why did the rivalries between England and Spain lead to war in 1588?

When the Armada arrived the English and Spanish fleets fought for nine days in the English Channel, after which the Spanish anchored for a week off Calais because they needed fresh supplies. There they were attacked by British fireships and, in panic, many of the ships cut their anchors and headed out to sea. A six-day battle off the Kent coast followed during which many Spanish ships were sunk. After sailing off into the North Sea, both sides ran low in ammunition and the English turned back. As they sailed around Scotland and Ireland many Spanish ships sank, partly because of violent storms (those which had cut their anchors could not use them to ride out the storms) and partly because the maps of the time were inaccurate. At least 19 ships were wrecked off the Irish coast.

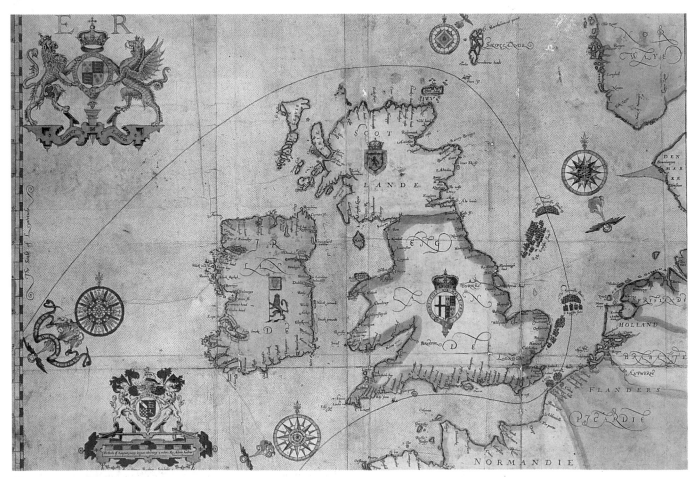

Source A

This map, published in 1590, shows the route followed by the 'Invincible Armada'.

● *What can this map tell us about the map maker's knowledge of the British Isles at this time? How does it help to explain why so many ships were wrecked off the Irish coast?*

Source B – The Launch of the Fire Ships, 1588
This painting shows the Armada and the British fleet.

Privateers

In the 1580s and the 1590s English privateers carried out about 100 raiding voyages each year. The main difference between privateers and pirates was that privateers gave some of the profits of their raids to the Queen. In return the Queen and her government turned a blind eye to their activities. Spanish treasure ships coming back from the Americas were the main targets for their raids. Spain complained bitterly about the activities of privateers like Sir Francis Drake but Queen Elizabeth unofficially encouraged them.

Source C –
Sir Francis Drake

● *What impression of Sir Francis Drake does this artist set out to portray?*

Religion

Queen Elizabeth's elder sister, Mary, had been a Catholic although Elizabeth was a Protestant like her brother, Edward VI. Mary had been married to Philip, the Catholic King of Spain, but had died childless. When Mary died, Philip asked Elizabeth to marry him but she refused. From that time on they were enemies and one of the matters which they disagreed about most strongly was religion. The Spanish ambassador to Elizabeth's court made many reports to Philip of the persecution of English Catholics. Philip believed that it was his duty to defend the Catholic faith and this meant that he wanted England to be ruled by a Catholic monarch. Elizabeth, on the other hand, believed it was her role to support the Protestant religion and saw herself as the head of the Church.

Source E – King Philip II of Spain

Source D – Queen Elizabeth I

This is one of the 'Armada' portraits painted by an unknown artist between 1588 and 1592

● *What impression of the Queen has the artist tried to create? How has he done this?*

The Netherlands

The Netherlands, which lay to the north of France and just across the Channel from England, was part of Philip II's Catholic Spanish empire. But some of his subjects in the Netherlands had become Protestant. In the 1560s there were a number of rebellions in the Netherlands against Spanish rule. Philip became more and more worried that the rebels might look for help from nearby Protestant England but Elizabeth was reluctant to get involved in a conflict which would cost her money. Eventually, however, Elizabeth was persuaded to help the rebels in the Netherlands in their fight with Spain.

In 1585 she sent them money and arms, which helped Philip make his decision to try to invade England and remove Elizabeth from the throne.

Ireland

Ireland remained a Catholic country even though Henry VIII and Edward VI had tried to introduce the Protestant religion. Elizabeth continued her father's policy of increasing English control of Ireland. Many of the Irish clan leaders, fearing they would lose their lands, turned to Philip of Spain and to the Pope for help, and Spanish and Papal troops were sent to Ireland on a number of occasions. As relations between England and Spain became strained, Elizabeth, fearing that Philip might use Ireland as a base from which to attack her, became convinced that she must bring Ireland under the full control of the Crown.

Source F – Mary Queen of Scots

Mary Queen of Scots

Mary Queen of Scots was Elizabeth I's Catholic cousin. By the time she became Queen of Scotland many Scottish nobles had become Protestant so Mary had many problems trying to establish her authority in Scotland. Eventually she fled to England in 1568 to seek help from her cousin Elizabeth but instead of helping her, Elizabeth made Mary a prisoner.

Elizabeth was afraid to release the Scottish Queen because she feared that English Catholics might try to get help from Spain to put Mary on the throne of England and make it a Catholic country again. Mary appealed many times to Philip of Spain for help. As early as 1565 Philip wrote: 'The Pope and I will consider the way in which we may aid the cause of God which now the Queen of Scotland upholds, since she is the gate by which religion must enter the realm of England.'

There were a number of plots to free Mary and put her on the throne but in 1587 Mary Queen of Scots was found guilty of plotting against Elizabeth and she was executed. Philip was said to be furious.

1 Copy the table below and complete it using all the information in this unit.

Reasons for tension between England and Spain	Type of reason (economic, political or religious)	How did this lead to war?
Privateering Colonies The Netherlands Mary Queen of Scots Ireland Religion		

2 Consider the situation which was building up between England and Spain from:
a Elizabeth's point of view;
b Philip's point of view.
Describe the situation from each point of view, explaining why one might blame the other for causing war.

3 Construct a time-line and mark on it all the major events of the period you have just studied. Make a list of the changes which took place during this period and whether those changes came about quickly or gradually. Make a similar list of things which remained unchanged.

Tudor policy in Ireland

1 Ireland in the 16th century

Two main groups of people lived in Ireland in the 16th century: the native or Gaelic Irish and the 'Old English', who had come to Ireland in Norman times. Some of these English families had inter-married with the Gaelic Irish and had adopted many native Irish customs. Others, who controlled a small area around Dublin called the Pale, and who were sometimes called Palesmen, had remained more English. It was only in the Pale that English was spoken and English laws were followed. The rest of the country was ruled by the Gaelic chieftains and 'Old English' lords, many of whom spoke Irish and followed Gaelic law and customs.

2 The need to control Ireland

Since Norman times English rulers had paid very little attention to Ireland but the Tudors took much more interest in the country and sought to gain greater control of it. One of the main reasons for this was because Europe had become divided by religion. When Henry VIII broke away from the Church of Rome he became even more concerned about the danger that Ireland could be used as a base from which to attack England. He knew that to prevent this happening he needed to be able to influence the powerful Irish lords who might take sides with England's European enemies.

3 Tudor policies

Various ways of increasing control over Ireland were tried. Henry VIII tried to bring the Gaelic lords under the direct rule of English law by persuasion. His policy was named 'Surrender and Regrant'. During the 1550s a policy of 'planting' people who would be loyal to the Crown began in the areas close to the Pale. Mary Tudor used this policy, called plantation, to extend control outwards from the Pale into the midland counties of Leix and Offaly so that the English of the Pale would be protected from raids by Gaelic Irish clans. Elizabeth Tudor also used plantation to try to gain control of large areas of Ireland.

4 The Munster Plantation

In 1585 Elizabeth began a plantation of English and Scottish settlers on lands which had been taken from Old English families in Munster. The land was divided up and given to English 'undertakers' who were so called because they promised or 'undertook' to bring English farmers and tenants to settle in Munster. Sir Walter Raleigh, who later planned the first colonies in America, was one of the most important English landholders. The Munster plantation was not a success. In 1598 the Irish attacked the English settlers and many of them returned to England.

5 The Nine Years War in Ulster

Ulster was the last extensive area of Ireland to be brought under English control. From 1593 Hugh O'Neill, the Earl of Tyrone, and his followers fought against Queen Elizabeth to prevent the Crown from taking control of Ulster as it had done in Munster and the rest of Ireland. The war lasted for nine years and cost the Queen a great deal of money. Two weeks after Queen Elizabeth died, Hugh O'Neill made peace with the new King, James I.

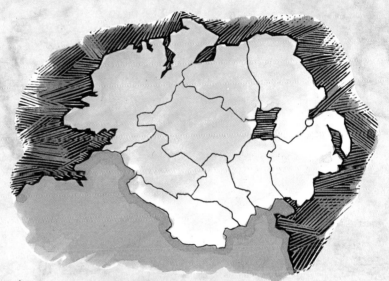

6 The Ulster Plantation

Some of his English enemies resented the fact that O'Neill and the other Irish lords were allowed to keep their land and, after the war, they tried to reduce the Irish lords' power. They succeeded because, four years after he surrendered, Hugh O'Neill and his followers fled to Spain. Their lands were claimed by the Crown and later used for the Ulster Plantation. It was divided up and given to English and Scottish 'undertakers' who promised to bring settlers to Ulster. The new settlers were mostly Protestant. Some belonged to the official Anglican Church – the Church of England. Others were Presbyterians and came mainly from Scotland.

4

Ireland in the 16th century

The English considered Ireland to be a primitive place. Tudor policy in Ireland aimed to make the native Irish, and the Old English families who followed Irish customs, 'civil'. They thought the Irish should become subjects of the British Crown and obey English rule. They should give up 'barbarism' and abandon their native way of life. They should learn to till the ground, live in settled communities and accept English laws.

What was Ireland like in the 1500s?

Landscape and people

Ireland was a mixed landscape of mountains, bogland, great woodlands and open farmland. In many parts of the country there were few towns and no roads. Travel was difficult except by river and by sea around the coast. The main inhabitants were the Gaelic Irish and the Old English, many of whom had adopted Irish ways and, it was said, had become 'more Irish than the Irish themselves'. There were also a number of Scots, the most important of whom were the MacDonnells, who had established a strong hold on North Antrim. They brought gallowglasses – professional soldiers who were paid to fight – to Ireland to fight in Irish wars. To expand their influence further they brought in Scots tenants in the 16th century. Attempts were made to drive them out but they managed to cling on to their land.

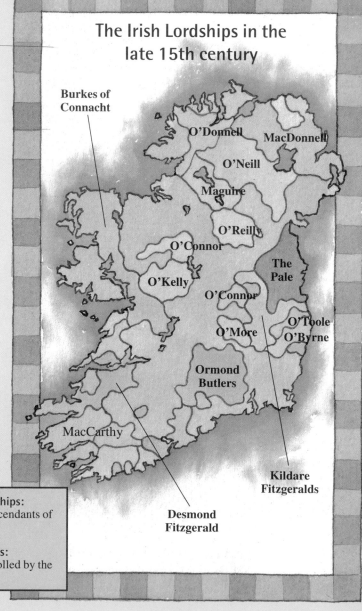

The Irish Lordships in the late 15th century

Burkes of Connacht · O'Donnell · MacDonnell · O'Neill · Maguire · O'Reilly · O'Connor · The Pale · O'Kelly · O'Connor · O'Toole O'Byrne · O'More · Ormond Butlers · MacCarthy · Kildare Fitzgeralds · Desmond Fitzgerald

Source A

This description of the ways of the Old English comes from an account of Ireland in about 1515:

There were more than 30 great captaines of the Englyshe noble folke that folowyth the same Iryshe order.

The State Papers of Henry VIII

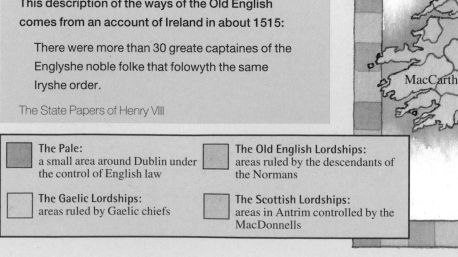

The Pale:
a small area around Dublin under the control of English law

The Old English Lordships:
areas ruled by the descendants of the Normans

The Gaelic Lordships:
areas ruled by Gaelic chiefs

The Scottish Lordships:
areas in Antrim controlled by the MacDonnells

Two languages, two laws

The main language spoken by the majority of the people was Gaelic Irish. English was spoken in the Pale but, even in areas loyal to English laws, Gaelic was the main language. Two sets of laws and lifestyles existed in Ireland side by side.

Most of the descriptions of Gaelic Ireland come from surveys made by English officials. Their job was mainly to gather information about Ireland which could be used by the army during wars or rebellions.

	English law		Gaelic Irish (Brehon) law
	Land, granted by the king to the lord, was passed on to the eldest son – the law of primogeniture.	**Land ownership**	The chieftain did not own the land; it belonged to the clan or family – the law of tanistry.
	Lords could inherit land and title. Criminal courts existed with judges who would order imprisonment or execution. Powerful lords had seats in Parliament but they were not elected. Land and property was mostly held by men.	**Laws**	Chieftains were elected from the leading families. Judges acted as arbitrators and could order offenders to pay compensation but they could not order imprisonment or execution. Clans gathered twice a year to make decisions. Women could own property.
	Mainly crop farming. The land was divided into villages and farmland. Wealth was measured in land and money.	**Farming**	Mainly cattle farming. Cattle were grazed on open land. Wealth was measured in the number of animals the lord owned.

Source C

The best evidence we have of how the Irish may have looked comes from a book called The Image of Ireland *written in 1581 by John Derricke, an Englishman who was in Ireland in the 1560s. This is a picture from that book and shows an Irish lord feasting after a cattle raid.*

Source D – Wilde Irish Man and Woman, 1616

Source E

This type of suit was worn in the 16th century. It was found on the body of a man which was excavated from Killery Bog, County Sligo.

Source F

Neill O'Neill dressed as an Irish chieftain, painted in the 17th century by John Michael Wright.

Source G – The clothes worn by a chieftain

He wore a coat of crimson velvet with aglets of gold, twenty or thirty pair over a great cloak of bright crimson satin girded with black velvet and a bonnet with a feather set full of aglets of gold.

The English Lord Deputy's description of Manus O'Donnell, an Irish chieftain, in 1541

1 Describe how the way of life of the people living in the Pale differed from that of people living in Gaelic regions.

2 Suggest reasons why so many descendants of the Norman lords lived like Gaelic chieftains.

3 Carefully study Sources B – G before copying and completing the table below for each source.

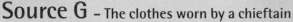

Source	Author and date	Evidence of Gaelic way of life and dress	Favourable or unfavourable impression of the Gaelic Irish?

4 John Derricke (Source C) is considered to be generally unsympathetic to the Irish but his book is still considered useful. Give as many reasons as you can to explain how and why historians of the period find it useful.

5 What evidence can you find that some English people despised the lifestyle of the Gaelic Irish? Why do you think these people had such a poor opinion of the Irish?

5

Early Tudor policy

England was setting up colonies in America at this time because of the great treasures of gold, silver and fertile land which that country possessed. Colonies or plantations were also set up by the English in Ireland.

Why did the Tudors want to gain stricter control over Ireland and how did they achieve it?

How Ireland was governed

The Norman king, Henry II, had been granted the right to control Ireland, under the title of Lord of Ireland, in a letter from the Pope – a Papal Bull – in 1154. The king usually appointed a Lord Deputy, chosen from the Old English lords, to rule in his name. Over time, as many of the Old English inter-married with Irish families and adopted Gaelic laws and customs, the Lord Deputy was left with less and less territory to govern in the name of the king and English power over much of Ireland declined. Eventually, certain of the big families even gained control of the office of Lord Deputy so the king's authority in Ireland declined still further.

Henry VIII and Ireland

When Henry VIII came to the throne in 1509 he was determined to regain stricter control of Ireland. His chance to get back his influence over the office of the Lord Deputy came when a rebellion, led by the Lord Deputy's son, was crushed by English troops. Henry had defeated the most powerful of the Old English families – the House of Kildare – and could now decide who should be the next Lord Deputy. He started to govern by direct rule, appointing officials from England to the post. Henry's aims were:

- to civilise Ireland by the spread of English laws and the English language;
- to bring the English Church into Ireland;
- to prevent Ireland from becoming a base for his enemies in England and Europe.

Source A – Henry VIII
This portrait, in the style of Holbein, was painted in the late 16th century.

In 1536 Henry declared himself Head of the Church in Ireland. England had already become a Protestant country following Henry's quarrel with the Pope over his divorce. Henry now made the English Church the official religion of Ireland. Catholicism was banned and Church land was confiscated.

Surrender and Regrant

The Parliament of Ireland, which was now under the control of his officials, invited Henry to become King of Ireland in 1541. He planned to gain control gradually by what he called peaceful ways and amiable persuasions'. He introduced a policy called 'Surrender and Regrant'. The Gaelic chiefs were persuaded to surrender their lands to the king but have them regranted, or returned, if they swore loyalty to him. Those who surrendered

Source B – The Surrender and Regrant Submission

and were regranted their land were expected to speak English, wear English-style clothing, follow English customs and respect English law.

One advantage of this was that under English law they gained the right to pass their land on to their eldest son. Under Irish (Brehon) law the land was owned by the clan and the leader had to be elected. By 1547, 40 Gaelic chieftains had declared their loyalty. Some chiefs were given English titles, for example the O'Neills of Ulster became the Earls of Tyrone. Although Henry gained greater control over some of the Gaelic lords, his attempt to introduce the Protestant Reformation did not succeed. The Gaelic chieftains remained Catholic and many continued to rule using Gaelic laws. Most of the people also remained Catholic.

—: The King :—
I will pardon chieftains who fought against me.
I will allow you to control your lands which can be inherited by your sons.
I will give you English titles.

—: The Gaelic Lords :—
I recognise Henry as Lord of Ireland.
I recognise Henry as head of the church in Ireland.
I will adopt English laws and language.

Source C

This is a modern verdict on the success of Henry's policy in Ireland:

> By the time of his death in 1547, Henry VIII's policy in Ireland had been largely successful. Not only had he destroyed the most powerful family in the country, the Fitzgeralds of Kildare, but he had also persuaded the Gaelic lords to submit to his rule.

G. Brockie and R. Walsh, *Focus on the Past: 2*, 1990

Plantations in Ireland

The control of Ireland was difficult to achieve by simply making new laws which were only obeyed in the Pale around Dublin. The Gaelic and Old English lords were independent rulers who often fought amongst themselves and had to be brought under English rule. One way to gain greater control over Ireland would have been to build forts and keep garrisons of soldiers but this would have been very expensive. Plantation was designed to give land to private businessmen, or adventurers, who promised to bring English settlers to Ireland and build defences for their protection. This saved the government money and troops but it also broke the power of the Gaelic lords and helped the spread of English control in Ireland.

This modern illustration, based on contemporary sources, shows the artist's impression of a plantation settlement.

The Plantation of Leix and Offaly

To protect the borders of the Pale, Mary Tudor authorised the plantation of the midland counties of Leix and Offaly which were renamed Queens County and Kings County. Soldiers and other settlers, mainly from inside the Pale, were given land to rent. Any contact with the native Irish was forbidden and the settlers had to build stone houses and keep arms to fight off attacks. This plantation did not succeed completely, due to a lack of settlers, but it was the first attempt and the mistakes were noted in future plantation plans.

Tudor and Stuart plantations in Ireland

Tudor plantations (1550–1603)

Stuart plantations (1609–1625)

---

1 What reasons did Henry VIII have for extending his control over Ireland ?

2 Name three changes that Henry brought about in Ireland.

3 Explain why Gaelic chieftains agreed to Surrender and Regrant.

4 Read Source C. Do you agree that all of Henry's policies in Ireland were successful? Explain your answer giving examples.

5 In a group, consider the following possible reasons for setting up plantations in Ireland:
- to spread the Protestant faith
- to gain gold and silver
- to make the growing English empire even more powerful
- to civilise the 'barbarous Irish' by bringing English laws, language and customs
- to prevent England's enemies from using Ireland as a base for attacking England
- to provide land and opportunities for English and Scottish settlers
- to make Ireland loyal to the English Crown
- to gain vast areas of fertile land
- to save government money
- to avoid wars with the Irish

Which does your group think are the most and least likely reasons why England wanted to set up colonies in Ireland? In each case try to explain your choice. Compare your group's lists with others in the class.

6

The Munster Plantation

During the reign of Elizabeth I, plantations were introduced on a larger scale.
The first planned and organised plantation in Munster, however, was a failure.

What were the rules of this plantation and why did it fail?

Disputes in Munster

In Munster, the ruling Old English lords had been fighting over land. While the dispute was being settled in London some greedy English adventurers took over land in Munster. The Munster families believed the Crown was trying to take control of their land and they rebelled. They obtained help from Spain and the Pope in their fight against the English and the Protestant religion but were defeated.

The Munster Plantation

By 1585, after crushing the Munster rebellion, the English government had confiscated about 480,000 acres of land in Munster. About half of this was good fertile land and the rest was of poor quality. Officials were sent out to survey and map the land. It was then divided into estates of between 4,000 and 12,000 acres. These estates were granted to English 'undertakers' who paid very low rents for this land. In return they undertook to plant it with settlers according to rules laid down by the English government.

● *Why do you think the undertakers were instructed to provide their settlers with weapons?*

● *What other precautions were undertakers instructed to provide?*

● *The undertakers were expected to pay the cost of carrying out these instructions. What effect might this have on the way the instructions were followed?*

Source A

Rules laid down for undertakers by the English government:

- Introduce English methods of farming on your land.
- Thirty English families are to be settled on a 4,000-acre estate.
- Provide your settlers with weapons.
- Provide your settlers with somewhere safe to go if under attack.
- Allow no Irish tenants on your land.

Source B

The worst sort of undertakers have done much hurt to the country and discouraged many from the voyage; for they have enticed many honest men over, promising them much but performing nothing, not even as much as to pay their servants and workmen wages. They demand for rent five pence an acre (they themselves paid only one and a half pence). They find such profit from the Irish that they do not care if they never settle any Englishmen there.

Robert Payne, *A Brief Description of Ireland*, 1590

Source C

And to speak the truth, the Munster undertakers were in great part the cause of their own fatal miseries. For whereas they should have built castles and brought over colonies of English, and have admitted no Irish tenant but only English, these and like agreements were in no part performed by them. The men of best quality never came, only those that made profit from the land. Others brought no more English than their own families, and all entertained Irish tenants and families that were now the first to betray them.

Fynes Moryson, Secretary to Lord Mountjoy, Commander of the English Army in Ireland, 1617

Source D – A modern view of the Plantation

It was aimed not at defence but to re-create the world of South-East England in Southern Ireland. English landlords would introduce English lifestyles by building villages, introducing the English law of landlord and tenant and English-style farming based on grain growing. Perhaps the most serious problem lay in the selection of landlords. Many did not have the cash to undertake the sort of plans the government had in mind.

R. Gillespie, 'Plantations in Early Modern Ireland', *History Ireland*, 1993

● *Examine Sources B, C and D carefully. What can we learn from these sources about the sort of people who became undertakers?*

Source E

Although there were many wise, godly and virtuous men yet there were out of England and other countries, traitors, murderers, thieves, runners-away with other men's wives, some having two or three wives, bankrupts and Papists.

The Calendar of State Papers for Ireland, 1598

What did happen in Munster?

The Munster Plantation began in 1586 and was successful for a time. A few English undertakers like Sir Walter Raleigh built up huge estates and became wealthy landlords. Some new towns were built and new farming methods were brought in. The land and climate were not as good as expected and the attacks by Irish raiders made life difficult and dangerous for settlers. In 1598 Hugh O'Neill, an Ulster chief, sent an army to Munster and by early 1599 the undertakers and most of the settlers they had brought over were driven out with great loss of life. By 1600 the plantation was in ruins.

---

1 The government plan was that the undertakers would bring over English families to farm in Munster. How can you tell from the sources that this did not always happen?

2 Compare Source D with Sources A and C.
a Decide whether each source is primary or secondary evidence, giving a reason.
b Find a statement in Sources A and C which supports the Source D statements.

3 Which source gives most useful information about the Munster plantation? Give reasons.

4 What evidence do we have that historians use primary sources when writing history?

5 Imagine that you are officials working for Elizabeth I. The year is 1600 and the Queen is disappointed by the failure of the Munster plantation. Write a report for Elizabeth explaining how and why the plantation went wrong.

7

The Ulster Plantation

Although, at the end of the 15th century, the English had established control of most of the rest of Ireland, their power in Ulster was still weak. Hugh O'Neill was one of the strongest lords in the area and was able to gather support from many other clans to resist the extension of English rule.

How did the Crown gain control of Ulster?

Hugh O'Neill and the Nine Years War

Elizabeth had made Hugh O'Neill Earl of Tyrone in 1585 thinking he would introduce English ways and laws into Ulster but instead he retained Gaelic laws and resisted every effort to interfere in his territory. This resistance turned into full-scale war in 1593. O'Neill had trained his army in modern warfare but he mainly used hit-and-run guerrilla tactics. After major defeats at Clontibret in 1595 and Yellow Ford in 1598, the English began to use a more ruthless 'scorched earth' policy of burning the land and thereby starving the people. O'Neill and his supporters were slowly encircled in Ulster.

In 1601, Philip of Spain sent 4,000 Spanish troops to assist O'Neill but they landed in County Cork instead of Ulster and were besieged by the English in Kinsale. O'Neill and his army had to march the whole way through Ireland to relieve them but they were defeated at the Battle of Kinsale and the remains of O'Neill's army struggled back to Ulster severely weakened and war-weary.

The Flight of the Earls

After surrendering in 1603, O'Neill was allowed to keep his lands in return for obeying English law. He had many enemies, however, among the English officials who felt he had been treated too leniently and who contrived over the next few years to reduce his power. Fearing plots against them, O'Neill and about 100 followers boarded a ship at Lough Swilly in 1607 and sailed from Ireland for the Continent. The 'Flight of the Earls', as it is known, left Ulster without leaders and their lands were taken by the Crown.

Source A
This modern painting by Tom Ryan shows the 'Flight of the Earls' in 1607.

When James VI of Scotland became James I of England in 1603 the position of the Scots tenants in Ulster became more secure. One of the first things the new king did was to increase the land owned by Sir Randall McDonnell who brought in new settlers from lowland Scotland. They were the first of a new kind of Scottish immigrant. Soon James granted more land in Ulster to lowland Scots. He gave James Hamilton and Hugh Montgomery of Ayrshire estates in County Down, which had belonged to a Gaelic chieftain, Conn O'Neill, so that the 'sea coasts might be possessed by Scottish men'. This is how the colonisation of Antrim and Down by mostly Protestant lowland Scots began. It prepared the way for the later official plantation of Armagh, Coleraine, Cavan, Donegal, Fermanagh and Tyrone which is known as the Plantation of Ulster. These remaining six Ulster counties were also to be planted with Protestant Scottish and English settlers. The scheme was aimed at removing the native Irish from these lands completely.

The settlement of Coleraine

Coleraine provides a good example of how the land was to be settled. The government granted the task to the great City of London companies of drapers, salters, fishmongers and haberdashers who undertook to bring settlers to the county. According to the plan, the land was to be granted by the City companies to Scottish and English settlers. The new settlers were not allowed to take Irish tenants although former soldiers, known as 'servitors', who got about five per cent of the land, were allowed to take Irish tenants. Ten per cent of the land was to be divided among the 'deserving' Irish who had been loyal during the Nine Years War but they had to pay the Crown double the rent paid by the soldiers. The native Irish were confined to the less fertile, hilly land.

Source B –

Map of Coleraine
This map and the plan of Coleraine on the next page were drawn as part of a survey of the Ulster Plantation in 1622. The king had discovered that the City companies were allowing many more native Irish people to occupy the land than was allowed in their contract. The survey brought to light many defects in the construction of the town of Coleraine and its fortifications.

Source C – Castle and bawn at Dungiven,1611

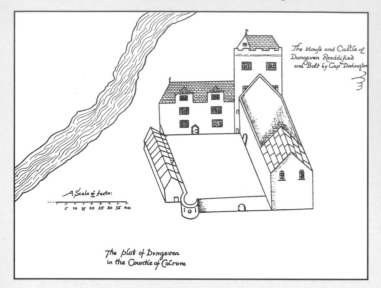

Each new owner of 1,000 acres was to build a defensive walled enclosure called a 'bawn'. Those who got 2,000 acres or more were expected to build a castle.

New towns in Ulster

The plans for plantation included the building of towns in Ulster. The design of these towns was based on military camps with defensive walls, a market square or diamond and streets running at right angles. Ulster towns may have been modelled on existing French towns. Some settlements were named after the company who set them up, for example Draperstown. The London companies added the prefix 'London' to the name of an existing settlement at Derry and renamed the county of Coleraine, County Londonderry, although the native Irish continued to use the old Gaelic place names like Doire or Derry.

Source D

The plan of the plantation town of Coleraine, 1622.

● *What evidence can you find in the plans of the plantation to suggest that the organisers were trying to avoid former failures? Refer back to the Roanoke and Munster plantations.*

Source E

This is an extract from a pamphlet by Thomas Blenerhasset in 1610. He was an undertaker who had received a grant of land in Fermanagh:

'…Art thou rich? make speed. Thou shalt do God and thy Prince excellent service. Art thou a tradesman? a Smith, a Weaver, a Mason or a Carpenter? Go thither. Thou shalt be high in esteem, and quickly enriched by thy efforts.
Art thou a Farmer whose worth is not over ten or twenty pounds? Go thither. Thou shalt whistle sweetly and feed thy whole family if they be six, for sixpence a day.
Art thou a gentleman that takes pleasure in hunt? The fox, the wolf and the woodkern [native Irish living in the woods and hills] do expect thy coming, and the comely stag will furnish thy feast with a full dish. There thou shalt have elbow room.
Art thou a Minister of God's word? Make speed, the harvest is great. Thou shalt see the poor ignorant untaught people worship stones and sticks.

● *Why do you think Blenerhasset published this pamphlet? What type of people is he trying to appeal to?*

● *Do you think he gives an accurate picture of life in Ulster? Give reasons for your answer.*

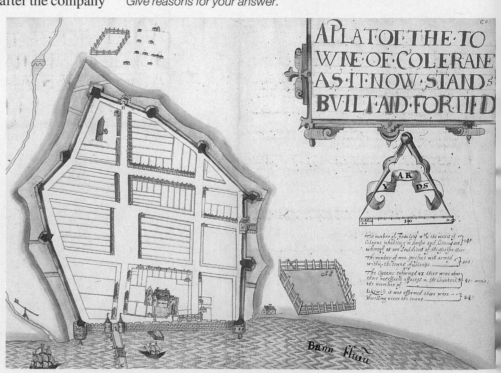

living side by side with the newcomers. Despite the strict rules which had been laid down, the London companies and others had allowed the native Irish to stay on the land because they needed them, either as labourers or as tenants who could be charged high rents.

Results of the plantation

- The English and Scottish Protestant settlement of Ulster was gradually established.
- Ulster, the last remaining Gaelic province, now had a mixed population of different and opposing interests and beliefs.
- The plantation was an economic success. More cattle and oats were sold to England and Scotland.
- Farming and building styles gradually changed.
- For settlers it was a success. They got good land, cheap rents and made profits.

Source F

Irish 'kern' soldiers in a contemorary drawing by a Belgian artist.

The Ulster Plantation was well organised; however, not everything was carried out as planned. It was expensive to bring over new settlers; by 1622 there were about 13,000 of them in Ulster. About half were Scots and half were English, but the Irish were still in the majority. Many of the Irish who lost their lands went to Europe to fight in Continental armies or to study in France, Spain or Italy. Some became outlaws, known as wood-kern because they hid in the woods and hills of Ulster and attacked the new settlers. But most remained on the land,

1 Explain in your own words how the land was to be divided between settlers, servitors and native Irish.

2 Imagine you are an undertaker with a grant of land in Armagh. Design a pamphlet to persuade settlers to join you. Explain in your pamphlet:
- why the plantation is taking place
- how it will be organised
- the sort of settlers who are needed.

3 What parts of the original plan of plantation were not carried out fully? What similarities are there with the Munster plantation?

4 List the many ways in which the new English and Scottish settlers changed the way of life of Gaelic Ulster. What aspects of life in Ulster remained the same ?

5 Describe how an Irish tenant might have felt about the plantation.

6 Construct a time-line and on it mark all the major events of the period 1566–1638 and make notes on how each event affected Ireland.

Conflict in England, Ireland and Scotland

1 The King and Parliament

James I, who had been responsible for the Ulster Plantation, was succeeded by his son Charles I. The new King believed that God had given him the 'Divine Right' to rule his kingdoms without calling Parliament. Over time, however, he had found it more and more difficult to raise taxes without Parliament's consent. In King James's reign, Parliament was becoming more strongly influenced by Puritans who were also opposed to the Established Church. The tensions between the King and Parliament increased.

2 Religion in Ireland after the plantations

Elizabeth I had passed laws in 1560 making the Protestant Church the official 'Established' Church of Ireland but most people in Ireland continued to practise the Catholic faith. The plantations, however, brought in many new Protestant settlers. Those who came to Ulster in the early 17th century tended to be either English Puritans or lowland Scots Presbyterians. These new settlers, as well as the Catholics, resented the right given to the Established Church to collect church tithes – taxes – from them.

3 Revolt in Scotland

Presbyterians in Scotland also resented the special recognition given to the Established Church. In 1638 a Presbyterian revolt broke out in Scotland against the King's attempt to impose bishops. The King needed Parliamentary support in the form of money to allow him to fight the war but his Parliament in England refused to grant him the money he needed.

4 Revolt in Ireland

In addition to resentment of the Established Church, many Catholic leaders in Ireland resented the plantations. The Gaelic clans had lost much of their land to English and Scottish settlers and the 'loyal Irish', who had been allowed to keep their land, had to pay high rents for it. In 1641 the clans decided to take advantage of the King's difficulties. They attacked the new settlers, murdering many of them. The revolt in Ireland was partly about religion but the real issue was land.

5 Civil War in England

In 1642 the tensions between the King and Parliament erupted into Civil War between supporters of the King, known as 'Royalists', and supporters of Parliament and its leader, Oliver Cromwell, who were known as 'Parliamentarians'. As in Ireland, the issues in England were partly about the practice of religion, but, more importantly, they were about the power of the King and how the country should be run.

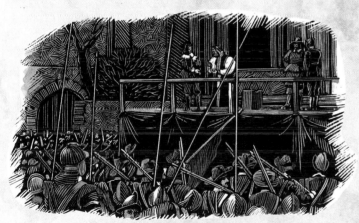

6 Taking sides in Ireland

The Gaelic Irish and Old English took the side of the King in the Civil War. Partly they hoped that he would give them their land back if he won, but they also feared what would happen to them if the Puritan Parliamentarians and their Scottish Presbyterian allies won. Most of the new settlers took the side of Parliament. The King and his Royalist followers lost the war and Charles I was tried and executed by Parliament in 1649. He was the only British ruler ever to be executed by his people.

7 Cromwell in Ireland

When the Civil War was over and the Royalist Army had been defeated, Oliver Cromwell went to Ireland to deal with the remains of Royalist support. Cromwell captured Drogheda and Wexford, where the Royalist garrisons were based, and many people were killed. Cromwell took the land from the Irish and gave it to Protestant landowners. Stories of what Cromwell did in Ireland have been interpreted as an attempt to punish Catholics for the atrocities of 1641.

8

King and Parliament in England

The struggle between King Charles I and his Parliament developed into Civil War in 1642.

Why did this happen?

Religion

The Church of England, or Anglican Church, had been established since Tudor times as the official English Church but many people felt it was too much like the Catholic Church. For example, both churches had much the same kinds of services and their ministers and priests wore elaborate vestments. Both had bishops and both sang hymns and played music at services. Harsh fines were imposed on those who did not conform to the 'Established' Church of England.

Puritans and Presbyterians

A movement to make the Church of England more strict and pure began to gain support in England. 'Puritans', as they were called, had ideas very similar to those of the Presbyterians in Scotland and Ireland. They were sometimes persecuted for their views and practices. The organisation of the Presbyterian Church differed greatly from both the Catholic Church and the Established Church. The Presbyterian Church had no bishops. Instead, the Elders were chosen by each congregation who, in turn, appointed ministers on behalf of the congregation. Each

congregation was responsible for its own affairs but it could send representatives to a General Assembly which made decisions for the whole Church in a particular area. Presbyterians were regarded as a threat to the Established Church. Presbyterian services, church courts and marriages were regarded as illegal.

Divine Right versus Parliament

The Stuart Kings, James I (1603–25) and Charles I (1625–49) believed that God had given them the right to rule the country as they saw fit and that Parliament was only there to help them. This way of ruling, which many monarchs of the time believed in, was called the 'Divine Right of Kings'. By the 17th century in England, however, Parliament had managed to increase its own role. The Crown generally had to get Parliament's approval for collecting taxes and spending large sums of money on, for example, war. Conflict arose when the king needed Parliament to grant him money. Parliament was reluctant to grant money unless the king gave it more say in the government of the country.

Charles I and his relationship with Parliament

Parliament did not trust Charles I any more than it had trusted his father, James. At this time an increasing number of Members of Parliament were Puritans. Charles therefore tried to rule without Parliament from 1629 until 1640, a period which was called the 'eleven years tyranny' by Charles's opponents.

The Short Parliament of 1640

When the Scots rebelled in 1638 Charles was forced to recall Parliament to ask for money. Then when the Irish rebelled in 1641 he had to try to get the support of Parliament to raise an army. But Parliament would not help Charles raise money until he dealt with their complaints. Charles refused and sent the Members of Parliament away. His army was beaten in Scotland and soon Charles had to call another Parliament to raise money.

The Long Parliament, 1640–1660

The Members of Parliament were better organised this time and they passed laws without the King's permission. Charles tried to arrest some of the leading Members but failed. Parliament began to take control of running the country and the MPs raised their own army. Charles gathered his supporters and the Civil War began.

Problems in three kingdoms

The King had three different types of religious and political problems in three kingdoms. The combination of these three sets of problems led to Civil War.

- In Scotland he had resistance from the Presbyterians to the imposition of bishops.
- In Ireland the Catholic Gaelic Irish were demanding their lands back.
- In England he had resistance from Puritans who wanted to reform the Established Anglican Church and have a stronger control over the King through Parliament.

Source A – Charles I

This portrait of Charles I was painted by Daniel Mytens in 1631.

Source B

The following message was sent by Charles I to Parliament in 1626:

I must let you know that I will not let any of my ministers be questioned by you. Hasten my taxes or it will be worse for yourselves; for if any ill happen I think I will be the last to feel it.

● *What evidence does this source give to suggest that Charles I believed in Divine Right?*

45

Britain during the Civil War seems to have been divided roughly between
areas that supported the King, and areas that supported Parliament.
Many parts of Britain saw no fighting at all, and most people did not join
the war. The biggest battle – at Marston Moor in 1644 – was fought by
about 30,000 people.

● *Where was the fighting concentrated?*

46

Who were the Royalists?

- many noblemen
- those who supported the Established Church
- most Catholics, who felt that the Puritans would be even more opposed to them
- the Gaelic Irish and the Old English in Ireland who hoped for their land back and who feared the Puritan/Presbyterian religion

Who were the Parliamentarians?

- Puritan MPs and their supporters
- Scots Presbyterians
- many gentlemen, merchants and townspeople who resented nobles
- many who lived in London and other large English cities
- the navy

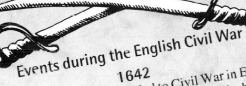

Events during the English Civil War

1642

The conflict with Parliament led to Civil War in England. The Royalists had some early successes. At the battle of Edgehill the King's cavalry was successful, but his footsoldiers could not defeat Parliament's footsoldiers. Between 1644 and 1646 Parliamentary troops began to defeat the King's troops. In 1645 Royalist forces suffered heavy losses at the battle of Naseby. The war was as good as over.

1646

The King was forced to give himself up to the Scottish Army.

1647

The Scottish Army handed the King over to Parliament. The King refused to agree with Parliament's proposals.

1649

The King was tried and condemned to death as a 'tyrant, traitor, murderer and public enemy'.

1649–1660

The Long Parliament continued to rule without a king.

---

1 What is meant by the 'Divine Right of Kings'?

2 Consider the situation which developed in 1642 from both the King's and Parliament's points of view. List all the reasons why each side would blame the other for causing the war.

3 Parliament today has much more power than the Crown. Using your knowledge of events in this period suggest reasons why this shift in power has come about.

9

Ireland in the 1640s

While Charles I was struggling with his Parliament, rebellion broke out in Ireland in 1641.
This rebellion was widely reported and many of these reports were exaggerated.

What caused the Irish rebellion and what is the legacy of the events of 1641?

Rebellion

The resentment of those who had lost their lands in the Ulster Plantation, or who now paid high rents for their land, came to the surface in 1641. Charles's troubles in Scotland and with his Parliament in England presented the Irish with an opportunity to overthrow the plantation and to win back their lands. A rebellion was planned to start on 23 October 1641 in Ulster and elsewhere. The plan was to take Dublin by surprise but English government officials in Dublin got news of this plan and captured some of the leaders the night before. The rising in Ulster, however, took place as planned.

The new English and Scottish settlers in Ulster were surprised and shocked as the Irish forces struck swiftly and fiercely. Many of the new plantation towns were captured. Settlers were driven out of their homes and villages and many were killed. Others were robbed and left homeless. Some of the more wealthy settlers were able to escape to England and Scotland but the less well-off were left to the mercy of their attackers.

The success of the Gaelic Irish in Ulster impressed the Old English. Although they were loyal to the Crown, as Catholics they feared the growing numbers of Protestant settlers and the growing strength of the Puritan Parliament. In 1642 the Gaelic Irish and the Old English came together and formed an association called the 'Confederation of Kilkenny'. The Confederation declared itself loyal to the King and against Parliament with the motto 'Ireland united, for God, King and Country!' What had started out as an attack on the new settlements, and therefore a kind of rebellion against the King, became linked with a struggle on behalf of the King and against those who supported Parliament.

Source A – Sir Phelim O'Neill

The following is a proclamation by Sir Phelim O'Neill, one of the Irish rebel leaders in 1641:

The rising is in noe wayes intended against our soveraine Lord the King, nor the hurt of any of his subjects, eyther of the Inglish or Schotish nation, but only for the defence and liberty of our selves and the natives of this kingdome.

Source B
A medal showing the motto of the Confederation of Kilkenny.

European connections

By 1642 most of Ireland was controlled by the Gaelic Irish and the Old English which was known as the Confederacy. They hoped to get help from the Catholic countries in Europe and in 1645 the Pope sent arms and money to the rebels. The Gaelic Irish forces were commanded by Owen Roe O'Neill, nephew of Hugh O'Neill. He had fought with the Spanish Army and, armed with the most up-to-date weapons, his troops defeated the Scottish Army of General Munro at the Battle of Benburb in 1646. Although this was a great victory for the Irish, the King's Royalist forces in England were defeated in battle over the next three years. By 1649, when the Civil War in England was over and the King had been executed, the Parliamentary leader Oliver Cromwell decided to come to Ireland to complete the victory.

Source C

James Butler, Earl of Ormond, the Lord Lieutenant of Ireland and the leader of the Royalist Party.

Years of unrest

The years between 1642 and 1649 were times of great unrest in Ireland. There were four armies which were not always under the control of their commanders:

- the Irish 'rebel' army, made up by Gaelic Irish, formerly loyal Irish landowners and Old English Catholics, led by Owen Roe O'Neill;
- the Royalist Army, led by the Earl of Ormond, based in Dublin;
- the Parliamentary Army, supported by the Scottish and most of the English settlers;
- the Scottish Army, led by General Munro and also supported by the settlers and Parliamentarians.

Each side fought to influence the outcome of the war in England because they knew it would have a direct effect on them and on the situation in Ireland.

---

1 Use the information in this unit to work out which of the armies each of the following would have supported in the Civil War and why:

- a Scottish settler burned out of his home by rebels;
- a formerly loyal Irish lord who paid high rents for the land he had been allowed to keep in Ulster, but who had now become bankrupt;
- an English settler who is a member of the Church of Ireland;
- an English Puritan settler;
- a Gaelic Irish lord who had lost his land in the Ulster Plantation;
- James Butler, Earl of Ormond, an Old English lord.

2 Use the information in this section to complete the table below:

Groups	Their reason for rebellion
Old English	
Gaelic Irish	
'Loyal' Irish	

3 'The Irish rebelled in 1641 only because Charles I was in trouble.'

Do you agree with this statement? Whatever your view, give reasons for your answer.

10

1641: examining the evidence

Early reports of the 1641 rebellion told of the massacre of thousands of settlers by the rebel Irish. The reports created shock waves in England and Scotland and the memory of these atrocities has been passed down in Protestant folklore.

What evidence exists to show whether a planned massacre took place and how reliable are the accounts that have been written about 1641?

The evidence from 1641

Most accounts of events in 1641 rely on two types of primary sources from the time:

● the 1641 depositions which amount to 32 volumes of statements made by Protestant settlers, detailing property they lost and sometimes describing atrocities;

● pamphlets and pictures designed to prove that a massacre of Protestants was planned and carried out by the rebels.

Source A – Deposition of Edward Slake of County Fermanagh

Edward Slake, of Gorteen in ye parish of Kinaly, County Fermanagh being duly sworn saith that on or about the 24th of October last, past about 10 o'clock in the forenoon he was robbed of and lost – viz:

	£	s	d
in corne which he paid for a week before	1	13	4
for cattle to the value of	60	0	0
for books	20	0	0
for bonds and bills due from English and Irish	8	14	0
for household stuff	20	0	0
for ready money	4	12	0

By the means of Bryan M'Rory M'Guyre, Dun M'Thomas M'Guyre, Shan Vor and Divers others who called me a base Rogue when I offerred to resist them when they were taking my goods away. He further sayth that on 24th of October last the said rebels took his Bible, opened it, and laying the open side in a puddle of water lept and stampt upon it saying 'a plague on't, this book hath bredd all the quarrell'.

Sworn 4 January 1642, Edward Slake

Source B – Deposition of Robert Maxwell of Armagh

Robert Maxwell of Armagh gave evidence about his brother:

[he was dragged] out of his bed in the rage and height of fever and cruelly butchered. And his wife Grizell Maxwell being in childbirth, the child half born and half unborn, they stripped naked and drove her to the Blackwater and drowned her.

● *Do you think that the 1641 depositions give us reliable evidence?*

Propaganda pamphlets and pictures

In the years immediately after the 1641 rebellion, pamphlets and woodcuts were published telling the story of the massacre from the Protestant point of view. Some of them are shown on this page.

Driuinge Men Women & children by hund: reds vpon Briges & casting them into Riuers. who drowned not were killed with poles & shot with muskets.

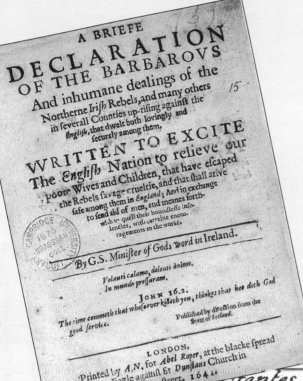

A BRIEFE
DECLARATION
OF THE BARBAROVS
And inhumane dealings of the
Northerne *Irish* Rebels, and many others
in seuerall Counties up-rising against the
English, that dwelt both lovingly and
securely among them,

WRITTEN TO EXCITE
The *English* Nation to relieue our
poore Wiues and Children, that have escaped
the Rebels sauage crueltie, and that shall ariue
safe among them in *England*; And in exchange
to send aid of men, and meanes forth-
with to quell their boundlesse inso-
lencies, with carraine encou-
ragements to the worke.

By G.S. Minister of Gods word in Ireland.

*Volanti calamo, doleuti animo.
In mundo pressuram.*

JOHN 16.2.
The time commeth that whosoever killeth you, thinkes that hee doth God good service.

Published by direction from the State of Ireland.

LONDON,
Printed by A.N. for *Abel Roper*, at the blacke spread Eagle against St *Dunstans* Church in Fleet-street. 1644.

◀ Source C –
A brief declaration

● *What was the intended purpose of this declaration?*

▲ Source D – Portadown Bridge

Source E

This woodcut carries the inscription:
English Protestants stripped naked and turned into the mountains in the frost and snow, where many hundreds perished to death, and many lying dead in ditches and savages upbraided them saying "now are ye wild Irish as well as we".

*...stantes striped naked & turned
...to the mountaines in the frost, & snowe, whe-
reof many hundreds are perished to death,
& many lynge dead in diches & Sauages
upbraided them sayinge now are ye wilde
Irisch as well as wee.*

The verdict of historians

Source F – A modern historian's view

I still find the depositions the essential source for the study of this period. It has become clear from my own analysis of the evidence that the hearsay reports of atrocities are unreliable, but even the most ghoulish of such stories is important. On the other hand I have found eye witness reports to be reliable and I have been able to check them for accuracy against the evidence of others who witnessed the same incidents.

Nicholas Canny, 'The 1641 Depositions', *History Ireland*, 1993

● *Why does this author think that 'even the most ghoulish of such stories is important'?*

Source G

Though the numbers were often fantastically exaggerated (one Protestant historian put the Protestant dead at over 150,000, more than the entire Protestant population of Ireland at the time) on balance historians seem to think that about 12,000 Protestant men, women and children were either murdered or died of cold and starvation in 1641.

Robert Kee, *Ireland, a History*, 1980

Source H

In October 1641, the Irish Catholics did rise all over Ireland at once: 200,000 persons were murdered.

R. Baxter, *Autobiography*, 1696

Source I

In 1892, W. E. H. Lecky wrote five volumes of *The History of Ireland in the Eighteenth Century*. This is a modern historian's opinion:

Later research has added little to Lecky's dispassionate analysis of the charge that a wholesale massacre of Protestants was planned as part of the rising. There was no such plan and no such massacre, but the rebels committed many murders, often savagely, because of lack of discipline, for vengeance or out of religious fanaticism, and there are many instances where Catholic clergy intervened to save lives.
The Protestant forces carried out widespread retaliatory massacres of the Catholics and, in Lecky's verdict, 'it is far from clear on which side the balance of cruelty rests'.

Patrick Corish in *A New History of Ireland*, Vol. III, ed. T.W. Moody, F.X. Martin and F.J. Byrne, 1976

---

1 Study Sources A, B and F carefully. Copy the grid and fill in each box.

	Is it a primary or secondary source?	What does it tell us about events in 1641? Give reasons.	Is it a valuable source of evidence?
Source A			
Source B			
Source F			

2 What impression and information about events in 1641 did Sources C, D and E seek to give ?

3 Why do Sources G and I give a different account of the rebellion compared to sources C, D, E and H?

4 How do you think a modern historian would try to work out whether any of the 17th-century sources can be trusted?

5 In groups prepare the front page of :
a a Protestant pamphlet from Ireland 1642
b a Gaelic Irish pamphlet justifying the rebellion of 1641
c a pamphlet giving the view of modern pupils studying the 1641 rebellion.

Compare the pamphlets and offer reasons to explain the different opinions of each group.

6 Discuss why such events might continue to have an importance for some people in Northern Ireland today.

Source J
– A 12 July Orange Order parade

Every year in Northern Ireland 'Orange Order' parades take place on 12 July to commemorate the Battle of the Boyne. Banners are carried which illustrate events regarded as important in Ulster Protestant history. One banner shows a picture of the incident in 1641 at Portadown Bridge. Banners such as these suggest that history and historic fears are very much alive for some Protestants in Ulster today.

SONS OF DOWN
L.O.L
Nº 1008

MY FAITH LOOKS UP TO THEE.

11

Cromwell in Ireland

Just as the 1641 massacres are an important part of history for some Ulster Protestants today, similarly the reports of Oliver Cromwell's atrocities in Ireland are an important part of history for Irish Catholics. His actions have been interpreted by some historians and some Catholics as proof of anti-Catholic brutality by the English.

Why should Cromwell be remembered in this way?
What legacy have his actions left in Irish history?

Why did Cromwell come to Ireland?

By 1649 Oliver Cromwell, the leader of the Parliamentary forces, had won the Civil War in England against King Charles I. The King had been executed and England had become a Republic – a state without a king. Cromwell declared himself Lord Protector of this new Republic from 1653 to 1658. He had many problems to deal with but the most immediate threat seemed to lie in Catholic Ireland, parts of which were still controlled by Royalist troops. When some of the Irish leaders gave support to the remains of the Royalist Army in Ireland, Cromwell decided to take his army into Ireland against them.

Cromwell's reasons for coming to Ireland were:

- to crush the Irish rebels;
- to reward those who had supported Parliament;
- to defeat the supporters of the King who controlled Drogheda;
- to take land for payment of his soldiers' wages.

Cromwell and Drogheda

Soon after his arrival, Cromwell marched with 10,000 troops to lay siege to the town of Drogheda. The Royalist garrison at Drogheda was commanded by an English officer, Sir Arthur Aston, and his troops consisted of a mixture of English Royalists and Old Irish soldiers. The town and its defenders had not taken part in the 1641 rebellion. The defenders of the town did

Source A – Oliver Cromwell
Oliver Cromwell arrived at Ringsend, near Dublin in August 1649. He had with him an army of 12,000 well-trained soldiers.

not give up easily and they fought long and hard against Cromwell's forces, refusing to surrender. Cromwell's soldiers eventually bombarded the walls and entered the town, plundering and killing the occupants.

Source B

This is an account of the capture of Drogheda by an English Army officer who was an eye witness of the attack on Drogheda:

As soon as Cromwell came before the walls of Drogheda he sent his trumpet player to sound an alarm call on those inside to surrender up the town. But they answered No. They would not surrender to such a notorious enemy of the King. After this Cromwell ordered his troops to bombard the walls with cannon fire. A few days later they made a breach in the wall. Twice Cromwell's men tried to enter through this breach but were beaten back with great loss. At a third attempt Cromwell himself led them but they had to fight hard in the streets. Once the Irish were defeated they were all cut down and killed and no mercy was shown to man, woman or child for 24 hours. Not a dozen people escaped out of Drogheda – townspeople or soldiers.

Source D

After stubborn resistance the garrison were driven into a church tower where they still refused to surrender. This is part of a report of what then happened, written by Cromwell to the English House of Commons after he had captured the Royalist stronghold of Drogheda:

Whereupon I ordered the steeple to be fired. The next day, when the other troops submitted, their officers were knocked on the head, and every tenth man of the soldiers killed, the rest were shipped to Barbados. I am persuaded that this is the righteous judgement of God upon those barbarous wretches who have soiled their hands in innocent blood; and that it will prevent the spilling of blood in the future.

Oliver Cromwell, 1650

● *Does this source provide evidence that Cromwell was taking revenge for the 1641 rebellion?*

● *What was the purpose of this report? How might that purpose have influenced Cromwell's story of the events?*

Source C

One of Cromwell's soldiers, Thomas Wood, gave the following account to his brother in 1674:

At least 3,000 people including women and children were put to the sword on 11 and 12 September 1649 in Drogheda.

Source E

A contemporary engraving of the attack on Drogheda

● *What do the sources tell us about the treatment of prisoners at Drogheda?*

● *Using all the sources write your own account of what happened at Drogheda.*

Cromwell's march through Ireland

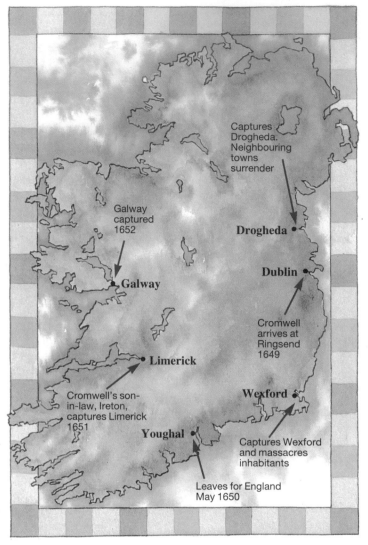

Captures Drogheda. Neighbouring towns surrender

Galway captured 1652

Drogheda

Galway

Dublin

Cromwell arrives at Ringsend 1649

Limerick

Cromwell's son-in-law, Ireton, captures Limerick 1651

Wexford

Youghal

Captures Wexford and massacres inhabitants

Leaves for England May 1650

Ireland after 1651

With the opposition defeated, Cromwell first had to deal with a large population which was homeless and starving. Much land had been destroyed and crops ruined or stolen during the fighting. Cromwell's solution was to round up the poor and the starving and sell them as slaves to work in the sugar plantations of the West Indies. He also hoped to crush the Catholic Church in Ireland by banishing priests and banning Catholic services like the mass. Irish soldiers who had fought against Cromwell left Ireland in huge numbers to join the armies of Continental Europe.

From Drogheda, Cromwell's Parliamentary Armies marched victoriously south through Ireland. Some surrendering garrisons were treated with mercy but Wexford was stormed while negotiating surrender. Around 2,000 are believed to have been killed including around 200 women and children who were slaughtered in the marketplace. By 1652 all Royalist opposition in Ireland had been crushed. Similar tactics were used in Scotland between 1651 and 1652 to crush some remaining Royalist opposition there. The Irish and Scottish Parliaments were abolished and so was the Anglican Church. Thirty representatives from each country sat in the Cromwellian Parliament.

What were the effects of Cromwell's land settlement?

To repay his soldiers and those landlords who had supported Parliament during the war, Cromwell took land from the defeated Irish landowners and gave it to his supporters and the new English settlers. Irish landowners were removed to the poorest land in the Province of Connaught, but many Irish remained as tenants of the new English landlords.

- Land in Ireland changed ownership from Catholic landlords to mainly Protestant landlords.
- Most of the tenants of Protestant landlords were not English settlers but Irish Catholics.
- Some of Cromwell's soldiers married into Irish families and became Catholics.
- Catholics lost land and property in the towns and were not allowed to take part in politics.
- Wealthy Protestant landlords ruled Ireland for many years to come.

The Cromwellian Plantations

Main area taken over by Cromwellian planters

The Mile Line. Only English soldiers were allowed to settle in this area

Catholic landowners transplanted to this area

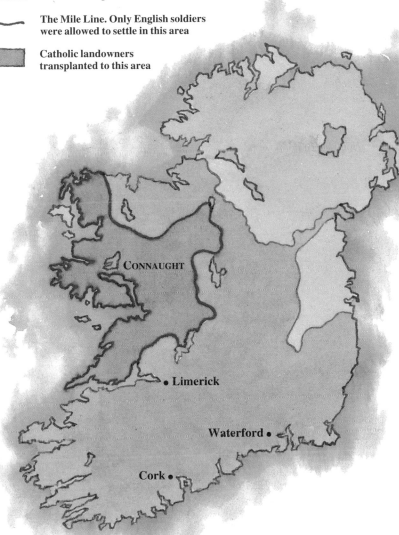

CONNAUGHT · Limerick · Waterford · Cork ·

Source F

His cruelty and ruthlessness have left a mark and a memory that the last 300 years have been unable to wipe out.

Veronica Wedgewood, 1958

Source G

By terror and evil land settlement, by banning the Catholic religion and by the bloody deeds [of 1649] Cromwell cut new gulfs between nations and religions. 'Hell or Connaught' were the terms he thrust upon the native Irish and they across 300 years have used as their keenest expression of hatred: 'The curse of Cromwell on you'.

Winston Churchill, *History of the English Speaking Peoples*, 1956

1 In what way did Cromwell's land settlement succeed and in what ways did it fail?

2 How do you think Catholics in Ireland at that time might have viewed Cromwell?

3 Study Sources F and G. On what point do both authors agree?

4 What evidence does Source G give to support the view that Cromwell's actions had a lasting effect on Ireland?

Kings in conflict

1 Charles II (1660–1685)

Oliver Cromwell died in 1658. In 1660 Charles II, son of the executed King Charles I, was welcomed back to England and restored to the throne as King. The Anglican Church was re-established as the official Church. This was known as the Restoration. Charles gave back to his Royalist supporters some of the land which had been taken from them during the Cromwellian period. But very few of the Irish who had lost their land during Cromwell's time got it back. Like his father and grandfather, Charles II did not get on well with his Parliament and he became increasingly unpopular.

2 James II (1685–1688)

After Charles II's death in 1685 his brother James became King. James's second wife was the sister of the powerful King of France, Louis XIV. She was a Catholic and James appeared to favour the Catholic religion more and more. Like his brother and father, he did not trust Parliament and Parliament did not trust him. In 1688 some Members of Parliament decided to replace him.

3 The Glorious Revolution

Parliament invited the Protestant Prince, William of Orange, to bring an army to England. William was married to Mary, the daughter of James by his first marriage. Both she and her husband were Protestant. James left England for France to seek the support of his father-in-law, Louis XIV. After he was gone, Parliament crowned William of Orange and Mary as joint rulers. This was called 'the Glorious Revolution'.

4 William III (1688–1702)

William was head of the House of Orange, and ruler of the Dutch Republic of the Netherlands. He was at war with the powerful Catholic King of France, Louis the XIV, who was trying to make himself all-powerful in Europe. William accepted the English throne in order to strengthen his position. He had to go to Ireland almost immediately because James had arrived there in March 1689 with French soldiers. James's intention in coming to Ireland was to get Irish help to get his throne back. James promised the Irish that if they supported him he would give them their lands back. Catholics in Ireland supported James. Protestant settlers in Ireland supported William.

5 The war in Ireland 1689–1691

William and James fought each other in Ireland for the right to the throne, but this war was also an extension of the bigger war in Europe against the power of Louis XIV. William defeated James at the Battle of the Boyne in July 1690. James left for France and William returned to England. William's victory at the Battle of the Boyne is celebrated every year by many Protestants in parts of Ulster and Scotland.

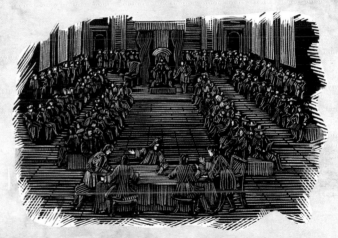

7 The Penal Laws

From the 1690s onwards Penal Laws were passed by the Irish Parliament which restricted the rights of Irish Catholics and Presbyterian dissenters: for example, a Catholic was not allowed to vote, become a teacher or be a lawyer; a Presbyterian was not allowed to become a member of a town council. The Penal Laws helped create a 'Protestant Ascendancy' (a ruling power group) in Ireland. By 1700 the proportion of land held by Catholics in Ireland had shrunk to 14 per cent and by the 1770s to about 5 per cent.

6 The Treaty of Limerick 1691

The Treaty of Limerick ended the Williamite Wars in Ireland. About one million acres of land were confiscated. The proportion of land held by Catholics shrank. Many Irish soldiers who fought for James in the war left Ireland never to return. They became known as the 'Wild Geese'.

12

The monarchy restored

In 1660, two years after the death of Oliver Cromwell, Charles II was crowned King and the monarchy was restored. This is known as the Restoration but in 1688, twenty-eight years later, Charles's brother, James, was removed from the throne by Parliament and William of Orange became King instead. This was called the Glorious Revolution.

Why did these events come about?

The Restoration of Charles II

When Oliver Cromwell died in 1658 there was no leader strong enough to replace him. Charles I had been executed in 1649, and in 1660 his son returned to England as King Charles II, promising to rule with the help of Parliament. Within seven years many people thought he had gone back on his promise. From around 1667 his opponents started to plot against him. A group of politicians, nicknamed the Whigs, tried to pass laws in Parliament to control his power and in 1679 they tried to pass a law which would prevent the King's brother, James, from succeeding him. When Charles dismissed Parliament the Whigs claimed he was behaving like his father and was trying to rule without them. Some of

them organised a secret plot to take over England. It failed and they had to escape abroad. Twenty years after the Restoration, England seemed to be as divided as it had been before.

Source A

Gilbert Burnet was made a bishop by Charles II. In 1690 he wrote this description of the King:

> He could be charming with anyone, but they could not tell when he was pleased or not. He was a chatterbox, who understood science well. He disguised the fact that he was a Catholic until he died. And he thought that any King who could be controlled by Parliament was not really a King.

Source B

The Restoration of Charles II in 1660. The procession moves from the Tower of London to Westminster. This late 17th-century painting is by a Dutch artist, Dirck Stoop.

British kings and queens

James VI of Scotland
(1567–1625)
and James I of England (1603–1625)
James was King of Scotland, England and Ireland. There were many arguments over money, power and religion during his reign. In 1625 his son Charles became King.

Charles I
(1625–1649)
In 1642 a Civil War broke out between Charles and Parliament. Charles lost the war and was executed in 1649.

Charles II
(1660–1685)
In 1658 Oliver Cromwell died and two years later Charles II was welcomed back as King. Soon, however, he became unpopular. He argued with his Parliament over power, money and religion.

Mary

James II
(1685–1688)
James was Charles II's brother and a Catholic. He was as unpopular as Charles II. Parliament decided to replace him. In 1688 they asked William of Orange to be King of England.

William III
(1688–1702)
Parliament made William and his wife Mary joint rulers in 1688. They made it against the law for a Catholic to inherit the throne. Parliament was to control taxes and the King was to be in charge of the army.

– married –

Mary
(1688–1694)
Mary ruled with William until her death in 1694.

Anne
(1702–1714)

James

Source C – James II

This portrait of James II was painted by Sir Godfrey Kneller in about 1684-5

James II became King in 1685 but he was very unpopular with many Protestant politicians who did not trust him because:

- he was a Catholic;
- he kept a large army;
- he had Catholic officers in his army;
- they thought he was trying to make England a Catholic country;
- he appointed the Earl of Tyrconnell, a Catholic, as his Viceroy in Ireland – Tyrconnell tried to undo some of the Cromwellian land settlement;
- in June 1688 his wife had a son who was baptised a Catholic and who would be the next king.

Parliament takes action

The English Parliament became more and more fearful of James. They believed he was trying to make England a Catholic country. Secretly they asked William III of Orange, the Protestant ruler of the Netherlands, to become King. William agreed to accept the Crown partly because he was having trouble with his great enemy, Louis XIV of France, and was hoping for an English army to help him fight Louis.

The Glorious Revolution 1688

William landed in England on 5 November 1688 with a large army. James fled to France for help. William and Mary were crowned as King and Queen but they had to agree to a Bill of Rights which made Parliament more powerful in England. Unlike the Civil War, this change in the way the country was to be governed took place without bloodshed and became known as the 'Glorious Revolution'.

Declaration of Rights
1689

yes I'm a Catholic

then you can't vote

No Catholic can become King.

Catholics cannot vote.

Parliament decides on laws and taxes, not the King.

Parliament keeps a check on the army.

The Bill of Rights limited the power of the monarch and increased the influence of Parliament. The king or queen could not interfere in Parliament's affairs or elections, could not change laws made by Parliament, had to allow Parliament to meet and to hold elections at least every three years.

1 Why was Charles invited to become King in 1660?

2 What did Charles II think about Parliament? How does this help explain why people plotted against him?

3 Complete the following sentences:
- James II brought about his own overthrow because…
- The English Parliament overthrew the King because…
- William agreed to accept the throne of England because…

4 Why do you think the events of 1688 were described as 'glorious'? Whose point of view does such a description represent?

5 How might supporters of James II and the 'Divine Right of Kings' describe the Bill of Rights of 1689 and why?

13

Ireland, England and Europe in 1688

The war in Ireland, which took place between 1688 and 1691, was the result of a coming together of a number of connected factors – British, European and Irish. In 1688 war broke out in Europe between France and an alliance of European rulers led by William III. This war lasted until 1697.

Why did Ireland become the battleground of Europe in 1688?

The situation in Europe in 1688

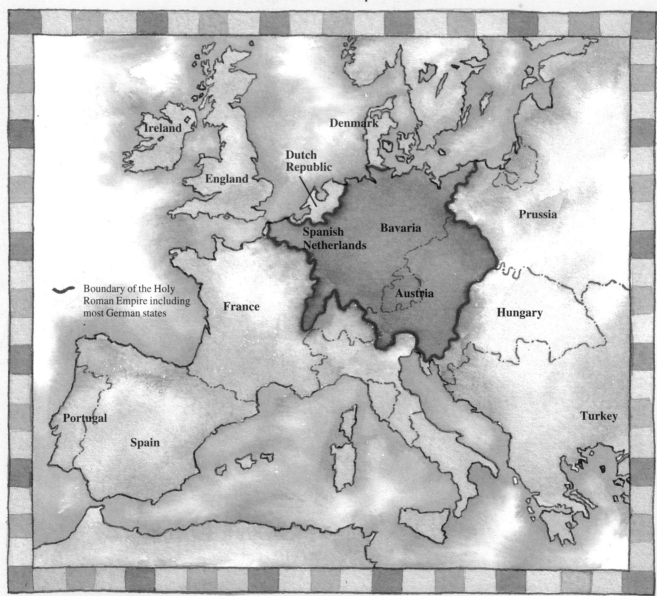

Ireland

Denmark

Dutch
Republic

England

Prussia

Spanish
Netherlands

Bavaria

Boundary of the Holy
Roman Empire including
most German states

Austria

France

Hungary

Portugal

Turkey

Spain

Source A -
Louis XIV of France

● *What impression does this painting give of Louis?*

Louis XIV of France

In the reign of Louis XIV (1647–1715) France was the most powerful country in Europe and Louis wanted to make it even more powerful by bringing the Netherlands and parts of Germany under his control. He also had ambitions in Italy, which so angered the Pope, who was the ruler of parts of Italy, that he threatened to excommunicate Louis. His ambitions also brought him into conflict with other European rulers. They felt threatened by him and created a Grand Alliance against him.

The Grand Alliance against Louis XIV of France

The Alliance against Louis XIV consisted of:

● King Carlos of Spain
● the Emperor Leopold of Austria, who also ruled many of the German states
● the ruler of Prussia
● the ruler of Bavaria
● William III, Prince of Orange
● Pope Innocent II, who ruled parts of Italy.

● *Find these countries on the map.*

Louis' plan

● to help James regain his throne by supporting him in Ireland
● to keep William occupied with the fighting in Ireland for as long as possible
● to use the conflict in Ireland as an advantage over the Grand Alliance which opposed him in Europe

William's plan

- to send an army to Ireland to defeat James
- to seek a quick victory and return to his main concern – the war in Europe against Louis

Prince William of Orange

Prince William III of Orange was head of the Dutch Republic in the Netherlands, a state which was in constant danger of being overrun by the French. In 1682 Louis XIV seized the Principality of Orange in south-eastern France, of which William was the ruler. In 1685 he took away the freedom previously granted to French Protestants and attempted to expel them and in 1688 he prepared to conquer the Dutch with the help of James II. William knew that most English people feared the growth of French power and did not approve of James's alliance with Louis XIV. William believed that the best way of protecting the Dutch Republic was to encourage the English to get rid of James II. So it was that he put together the Grand Alliance of European States and accepted the throne of England.

James II

James II wanted to rule with complete power. He was prepared to consult Parliament but not to obey its decisions. After Anne Hyde, his first wife, died he married Mary of Modena, a deeply religious Catholic and friend of both the Pope and Louis XIV. This marriage showed most English people that James would ally England with France and make it a Catholic country again.

When James II began to recruit an army in Ireland, Members of Parliament at Westminster were alarmed: those troops could be used against Parliament and to help Louis against the Dutch Republic. English aristocrats invited William to help them and a large Dutch army landed at Brixham in November 1688. James did not resist and fled to France. William became joint ruler of England, Scotland and Ireland with his wife, Mary, who was the eldest daughter of James II. The only hope James had of getting his throne back was with the help of the Catholic Irish. In March 1689, James landed at Kinsale, County Cork, with a large French army. The war to decide the future of Ireland, Scotland, England and much of the rest of Europe had begun.

James's plan
- to raise an army in Ireland with French help
- to defeat William's supporters in Ireland
- to use Ireland as a stepping stone to regain his throne in England

Ireland in 1688

During his short reign James had been gradually improving the position of Catholics in Ireland. He had appointed a Catholic, the Earl of Tyrconnell, as his Viceroy. This alarmed Protestants in both England and Ireland. He gave Catholics positions as judges, town councillors and army officers. The Gaelic Irish and the Old English hoped James would restore their lost lands and their position of power.

Protestant fears

The Protestants feared that what had happened in 1641 would be repeated. Many settlers fled to England and Scotland when rumours spread of attacks on Protestants by James's supporters – the 'Jacobites'. Protestant landowners in the north began raising troops from among the settlers who remained. They declared their support for King William and sent messages asking for his help.

War in Ireland

The Catholics of Ireland, both the Old English and the Gaelic Irish, gave James II a great welcome and the French Army marched north to Dublin with no opposition. Those Catholics who had lost land during the Ulster Plantation and after Cromwell had overrun Ireland now hoped to get it back again.

Protestant landlords of Ulster not only asked for William's help but decided to resist the 'Jacobites', the supporters of King James. The Protestant Army, however, was completely beaten at Dromore, County Down, on 14 March 1689. The Jacobites plundered Hillsborough, Lisburn and Antrim and occupied Belfast without difficulty. The forces loyal to King William decided that they could resist the Jacobites at two points only: Londonderry and the island town of Enniskillen. James did not particularly care about the Irish or their problems but he did allow his Irish Parliament to discuss how previously lost land could be given back. William was not really concerned with the Irish people either: he was on Irish soil only to defeat James and the French, just as James's main concern was to use Ireland to get back his throne.

---

1 Which European countries and rulers supported:
a William in Ireland in his battle against James?
b James in Ireland in his battle for the English throne?

2 Briefly explain why James and William both came to be in Ireland in 1690.

3 Draw a flow diagram to show how Ireland became involved in a European war.

14

Two Kings in Ireland, 1689–1691

Some of the events of the 'War of the Two Kings', such as the Siege of Derry
and the Battle of the Boyne, are commemorated still today.

What happened at Derry and the Boyne and what legacy have these events left behind?

No Surrender: The Siege of Derry 1688–89

When James II arrived in Ireland in March 1689 most of the country was under the control of his supporters – the Jacobites. James's plan was to march north, crush the Williamite supporters in Ulster, link up with Scottish Jacobites and invade England.

The first obstacle to James's plan was the plantation town of Londonderry which had declared in favour of William. What began as a local dispute dramatically became a part of the 'War of the Two Kings' and the larger European war in which they were involved. The city was a planned plantation town, surrounded by stout defensive walls. Access into it was through four strong gates which could be closed against enemies in times of danger. The city was inhabited mainly by Protestant settlers. Catholics lived outside the city walls in an area of hollow, marshy land known as the Bogside.

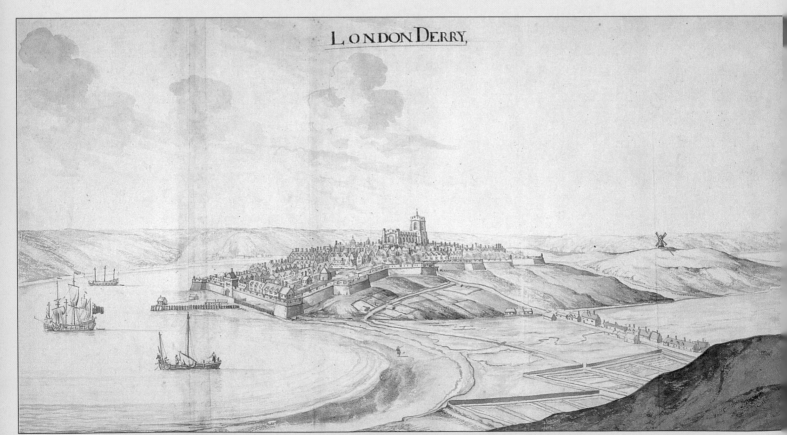

Source A – Londonderry
This view was probably prepared for Charles II before 1685 when he was considering strengthening the fortifications of the city.

Source B – The Siege of Derry, 1689

This Dutch print does not show the landscape very accurately but does give a good impression of the stength of the bombardment.

Shutting the gates

James II and the Earl of Tyrconnell replaced the Protestant corporation which governed the city with a mainly Catholic one. The Protestant troops guarding Londonderry were sent to Dublin and were to be replaced by a Catholic garrison. The Protestants feared another Catholic rising like 1641 and many Protestants from surrounding areas flooded into the city for protection. When the Catholic troops arrived 13 young apprentice boys shut the gates of the city against them. The people of the city were promised that support would be sent by the new King William and when James returned to Ireland and arrived at the city walls, the Protestant defenders refused to surrender.

The Siege

The Jacobite Army had no siege guns but used mortars to damage buildings in the city. The River Foyle was blocked to shipping by a boom which stretched across the river so that relief ships could not reach the city. The aim was to starve the citizens into surrender and the siege continued for many weeks.

Source C – The boom

They contrived to place a boom of timber, joined by chains and cable 12 inches thick. It was fastened at one end through the arch of a bridge and at the other by a piece of timber forced into the ground.

George Walker, *A True Account of the Siege of Londonderry*, 1689

Source D – Conditions inside and outside the city

Conditions soon became very difficult for the defenders and citizens inside the walls of the city. The weather was very wet and many people had to sleep in the open. Many were sick or wounded but food was the greatest problem. The following extracts from accounts written by survivors give some idea of the hardships endured:

Our women also did good service at the Bogside, in beating off with stones the soldiers who came to our lines.

John MacKenzie, *Narrative of the Siege of Londonderry*, 1690

June–July 1689
We were under so great need, that we had nothing left unless we could prey upon one another.
A certain fat gentleman conceived himself in the greatest danger and fancying several of the garrison looked on him with a greedy eye thought fit to hide himself for three days. Our drink was nothing but water, which we could not get without danger. We had to eat tallow [candles] and starch which did nourish and support us.

George Walker, *A True Account of the Siege of Londonderry*, 1689

4 June 1689
We are in greater danger by [the bombs] thrown in the day, it being more difficult to see them. The dread of them forced our people to lie about the walls and to go to the places remotest from houses. And the cold, especially for the women and children, added to their want of rest and food, caused diseases and fevers of which great numbers died.

Food price list during the siege

	s	d
Horse flesh per pound	1	8
A dog's head	2	6
A cat	4	6
A pound of tallow	4	0
A pound of salted hides	1	0
A pound of horse blood	1	0
A rat	0	6
A mouse	0	6
A horse pudding	0	2
An handful of sea wreck	0	1
An handful of chickweed	1	0
A quart of meal when found	5	6
A quarter of a dog (fattened by eating the bodies of the slain Irish)		

The end of the siege

Outside the city the Jacobites also suffered great hardship. They had poor weapons, were also lacking food and had few medical supplies for the wounded. Humiliated by the determination of the defenders, many deserted. On Sunday 28 July 1689, Williamite ships broke through the boom on the river and sailed up to the city, despite cannon fire from both banks. The inhabitants were jubilant. Three days later the Jacobites withdrew and the Siege of Derry, which had lasted for 105 days, ended. The failure to take Derry and also the town of Enniskillen was a bitter disappointment to James and his army. He had not gained control of Ulster as he had hoped, so he returned south.

Source E – The Battle of the Boyne, July 1690

Painted by Jan Wyck in 1690.

William landed at Carrickfergus on 14 June 1690 and marched south. Never before had Ireland seen such a large army – perhaps 36,000 in all, including Dutch, English, Scots, Danes and French Protestants. The Jacobite Army was around 25,000 strong and also contained troops from many countries. The Jacobites had chosen to fight at the River Boyne north of Dublin where the two armies met on 1 July.

Source F

The Boyne was a significant rather than a great battle. As a result of it William won Dublin and Leinster and more than half of Munster – priceless advantages. It was regarded as a great victory by that part of Europe that opposed Louis XIV of France. Militarily the Boyne was the decisive battle of the war in Ireland.

G. A. Hayes-McCoy, *Irish Battles, A Military History of Ireland*, 1969

The Boyne is the most famous battle in Irish history but it was actually much smaller and there were far fewer casualties than later battles such as Aughrim. Nevertheless, William's victory at the Boyne forced James to flee back to France, never to return again.

Source G

On the morning of 1 July, 10,000 Williamite troops led by Heinhardt Schomberg, the Duke of Schomberg's son, marched up river to Rosnaree on the River Boyne. Tyrconnell, the Jacobite commander, was sure that the main threat would come there and so he moved more than half his army in that direction. This allowed the main body of the Williamite army to wade across the river (at Oldbridge). The Jacobites were outnumbered and forced to retreat in confusion. It is estimated that some 1,000 Jacobites were killed and about half that number of Williamites.

T. Parkhill, *History Ireland*, Spring 1993

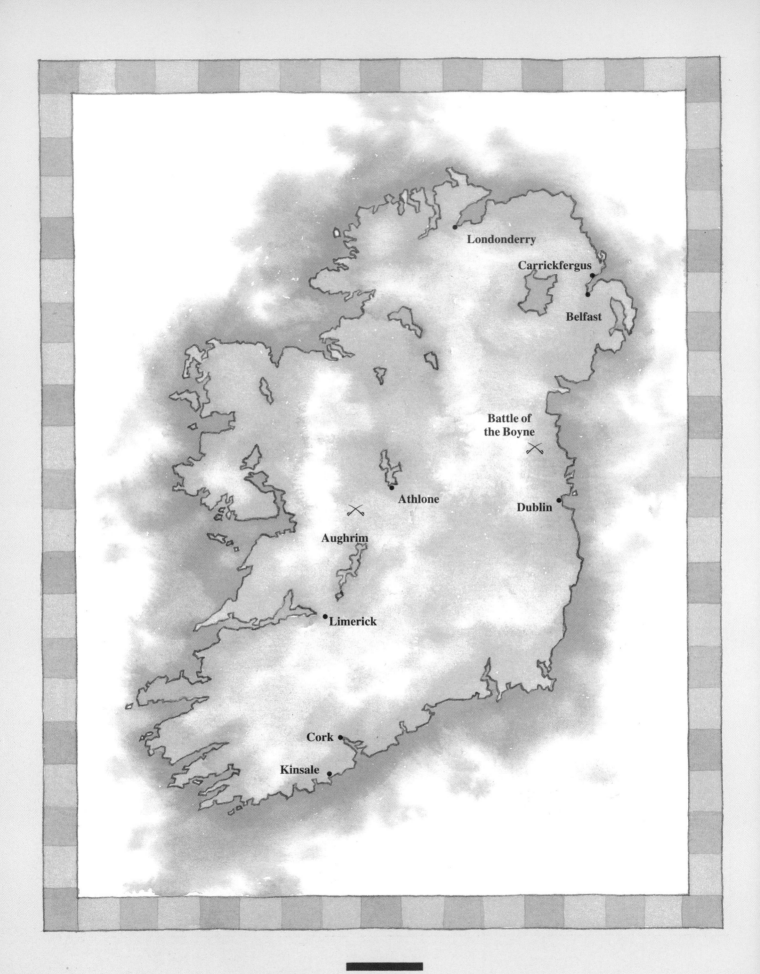

Londonderry

Carrickfergus

Belfast

Battle of
the Boyne

Athlone

Dublin

Aughrim

Limerick

Cork

Kinsale

The main events of the Williamite wars

March 1689
James lands at Kinsale

April–July 1689
Londonderry, which is in the hands of Protestant
settlers, is laid siege by James

June 1690
William lands at Carrickfergus

July 1690
William defeats James at the Boyne.
James flees to France

September 1690
William's Army captures Cork

June 1691
William's Army captures Athlone

July 1691
William's Army wins Battle of Aughrim

September–October 1691
The Siege of Limerick

October 1691
Jacobites surrender. Treaty of Limerick is signed

Limerick and Aughrim

The Jacobites escaped destruction at the Boyne and
under the command of Patrick Sarsfield, the Earl of
Lucan, the French and the Irish held a line of defence
along the River Shannon. In the Tipperary hills Sarsfield
and his men blew up many of William's guns. This was
later to help the people of Limerick to hold out when
their city was besieged in August 1690.

William of Orange returned to England and his army
was not able to cross the Shannon until June 1691. On
12 July the two armies met on the plains of east Galway
at Aughrim. The Jacobites were completely routed.
Aughrim was the bloodiest battle in Irish history: at least
7,000 were killed. When news of the victory arrived in
the north, the Protestants there lit bonfires in celebration
as they would do every 12 July after that.

The Williamite Wars remembered

The Siege of Londonderry and the Battle of the Boyne
are the subject of songs, banners and wall paintings.
Marches are held on 12 July each year to commemorate
the victory at the Boyne and on 12 August to
commemorate the relief of the Siege of Londonderry.
The Orange Order takes its name from William of
Orange but was not set up until a century after these
events had taken place. Members of the Order often
wear orange sashes when taking part in a
commemorative march.

Source H

The Sash My Father Wore symbolises the
continued importance of the events of 1689–91 in
Protestant folk memory:

It was old but it was beautiful and the colours they
*   were fine.*
It was borne at Derry, Aughrim, Enniskillen and the Boyne.
O me father wore it as a youth in the bygone days
*   of yore,*
And it's on the twelfth I love to wear the sash my
*   father wore.*

---

1 Imagine you were an officer in William's Army
bringing relief to Derry after the siege. Write a report
for the King describing:
- the reasons for the siege;
- the resistance of the defenders;
- the conditions in the city during the siege;
- the excitement felt at the relief of the city.

2 Describe the plan used by William's troops to
defeat the Jacobites at the Boyne.

3 What advantages did William gain after the Boyne?

4 a Examine Source H and use the list of events to
explain:
- why you think each of the places have been
mentioned;
- whether 'the sash' was actually worn at these
events.

b Why do you think the song makes a link between
these events and the Orange Order?

15

The legacy of the Williamite Wars

After his defeat at the Boyne, James fled to France. The Jacobite Army fought on in Ireland but eventually surrendered in October 1691. The Treaty of Limerick was signed on 3 October 1691 and was considered to be very fair at the time.

If the Treaty was fair why did the wars leave an enduring legacy of distrust in Ireland?

The Treaty of Limerick brought to an end nearly three years of fighting in Ireland. The Treaty was divided into two parts: the Military Articles, which affected the soldiers who had fought, and the Civil Articles, which affected the people.

Source A – Patrick Sarsfield, Earl of Lucan

The Military Articles offered the Irish Jacobite soldiers three choices:
* to return home in peace;
* to join William's Army and fight with him in Europe;
* to go to France.

About 5,000 soldiers led by Patrick Sarsfield chose to leave Ireland almost immediately and many more were to follow. They became known as the 'Wild Geese'. About 12,000 Irish Jacobite soldiers eventually fought in Europe as James's army. When peace in Europe came they joined the French Army and formed Irish regiments until 1789.

Source B

Ginkel [a Williamite Lieutenant-General also known as the Earl of Athlone] agreed that Sarsfield's Army could withdraw to France, which seems oddly generous but it prevented large-scale guerrilla resistance. This suited Sarsfield, who wanted to withdraw with his supporters to France, while many Williamites were astonished that they ended up shipping a large army gratis [free] to Louis XIV.

R. F. Foster, *Modern Ireland 1600–1972*, 1988

The Civil Articles promised that the Irish who had supported James would not lose their land and would be allowed to practise their religion freely. Only the land belonging to those who had been killed or who had fled, which amounted to 1 million acres, was to be confiscated.

Decline in Catholic land ownership

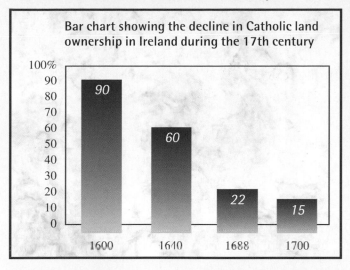

Bar chart showing the decline in Catholic land ownership in Ireland during the 17th century

The Penal Laws

The Treaty of Limerick was viewed by many as tolerant and fair under the circumstances. But soon after William left Ireland the Irish Parliament passed a series of Acts to restrict the religious and political freedom of Catholics and Protestant dissenters, such as the Presbyterians and Quakers. The Penal Laws were passed by a Protestant Parliament made up of Church of Ireland landowners and bishops who wanted to make sure the Catholic Irish, in particular, would be in no position to rebel again.

A list of Penal Law restrictions

- Catholic archbishops and bishops had to leave the country. If they returned they could be executed.
- One priest was allowed to remain in each parish but on his death he was not to be replaced.
- Catholics were forbidden to buy land from Protestants.
- Catholics were forbidden to vote in elections.
- If the eldest son of a Catholic landlord became a Protestant he could lay claim to all his father's land.
- When a Catholic landlord died the land had to be divided equally among all his sons, thus splitting it up into small farms.
- Catholics could not become teachers, doctors, lawyers, or officers in the army or navy.
- Catholics could not go to university or send their children abroad to be educated.
- Catholics were not allowed to become MPs.
- Presbyterians had to pay taxes to the Church of Ireland and Presbyterians could not hold services except weddings.
- Presbyterians were banned from town councils and official jobs.

Source C

The effects of the Penal Laws were not so serious as the terms of the Acts might lead one to suppose. For one thing, government was not all that efficient, for another Protestants were not agreed on the matter. More important, the courage of many Catholic clergy kept the vast majority of the people secure in their faith. The established church made no serious attempt to convert the Catholic population. The real purpose of the Penal Laws was to deprive Catholics of political power by controlling the ownership of land. Catholic landowners were the main victims.

Eileen Black, *Kings in Conflict*, Ulster Museum, 1989

- *Give reasons why you think the Protestant-dominated Parliament thought it was necessary to pass such laws.*

1 Categorise the Penal Laws under the following headings:
- laws against religion;
- laws against education;
- laws against civil rights;
- laws against property.

2 Offer reasons to explain why many of these laws also applied to Presbyterians and Quakers.

3 Either write a speech justifying the Penal Laws from the point of view of an Irish Member of Parliament or write a newspaper article about the injustices of the Penal Laws from the point of view of an Irish Catholic landowner.

4 Construct a time-line and mark on it all the major events of the period 1660–1700. Make a list of the major changes which took place during this period and whether those changes came about quickly or gradually.

16

From Penal Laws to Home Rule

In Cromwell's time, wolves were such a nuisance that they invaded the streets of Dublin.
A hundred years later these animals were rare and the last wolf was killed in the 1780s,
probably in County Carlow. The Irish countryside changed rapidly as the great
oak forests were cut down to build ships, make barrels and smelt iron.

*What other changes took place in Ireland in the century of peace after
King William's victories at the Boyne and Aughrim?*

Growing prosperity

The population rose from around 2 million in 1700 to nearly 5 million by 1800 as Ireland became more prosperous than ever before. As farmers moved into the wilder parts of the country to cut turf, graze cattle and grow corn and potatoes, so landlords could charge higher rents and build fine mansions such as Castletown in County Kildare and Castlecoole in County Fermanagh. Ireland was part of the British Empire and, as new lands were conquered overseas, so Ireland's trade grew rapidly and Dublin became the second largest city in the Empire.

Revolutionary ideas

New ideas came to Ireland along with the cargoes of cotton, sugar, wine and brandy from abroad. The outbreak of the French Revolution in 1798 caused great excitement in Ireland: if the people of France could get rid of their tyrants, perhaps the Irish could win their freedom too. The Society of United Irishmen, founded in Belfast in 1791, called for Irish independence and for a Parliament elected by all the people. The Irish Parliament, which represented only landlords and their relations, refused and rebellion broke out in 1798.

Source A

The Battle of Ballynahinch *by Thomas Robinson. During the rebellion, the French sent a small army to County Mayo to help the rebels. Though these invaders were defeated, the British government feared that France, or some other enemy, would join with the Irish and attack England from the west.*

Source B
The Irish House of Commons, 1780 *by Francis Wheatley*

The Act of Union

The Westminster government decided that Ireland must be ruled directly from London. In 1800 the Irish Parliament was persuaded to vote itself out of existence and the Act of Union came into force the following year. At first only a small number of people felt strongly either for or against the Union. The Penal Laws had been removed except for one important one: Catholics could still not sit as Members of Parliament in Westminster. A lawyer from County Kerry, Daniel O'Connell, led a peaceful campaign which eventually forced the government to grant Emancipation in 1829 and remove virtually all of the civil restrictions on Catholics, reinstating their right to be elected to the Parliament in London.

Famine

Meanwhile, the population was rising quickly and there were 8.25 million people in Ireland by 1841. Too many people were trying to survive by renting tiny pieces of land and around a third of them lived entirely on potatoes. Then in 1845 disaster struck: disease destroyed the potato crop that year and for several years to come. About 1 million people died of hunger and fever and another million left Ireland for other lands. The famine did much to persuade the Irish that they should be ruled from Dublin, not London.

Demands for Home Rule

By the 1880s most Irish people and a majority of Irish MPs were calling for 'Home Rule' but Irish Protestants, who represented about a quarter of the population, still supported the Union, especially in the north-east. Belfast had become Ireland's largest and richest city – a world-centre for the making of linen and the building of ships – and the Protestants of Ulster believed that their success was due to the Union with Britain. So it was that when a British government decided to attempt to give Ireland Home Rule in 1886, it was certain that there would be angry opposition from Ulster.

Source C – The famine
This picture appeared in the Illustrated London News *on 22 December 1849.*

17

Review: history or myth?

Many of the events which you have studied are 'claimed' by one tradition or another in Northern Ireland as representing past injustice or persecution.

How have the events of the 16th and 17th centuries, or the way these events have been simplified and distorted by Catholic and Protestant folklore, contributed to the emergence of two separate traditions in Northern Ireland today?

The dates and events identified below have been divided into those which are often claimed as part of the Catholic / nationalist tradition or the Protestant / unionist tradition and some of the 'popular' versions of these events have been described.

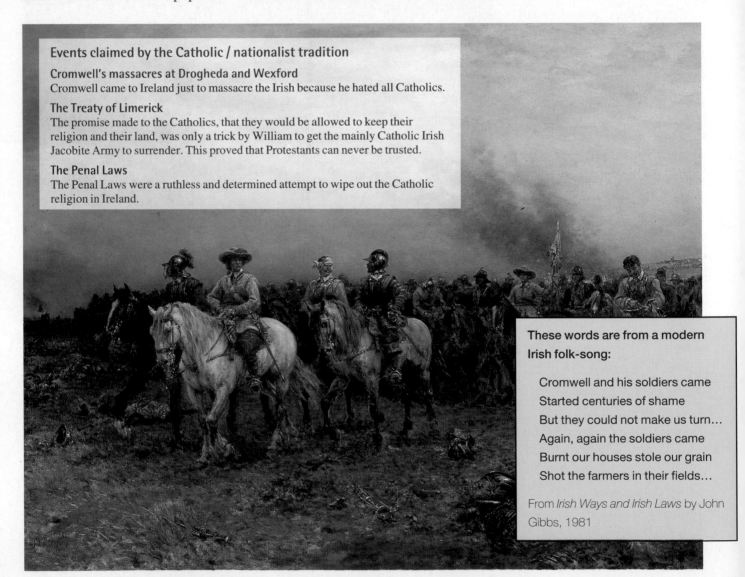

Events claimed by the Catholic / nationalist tradition

Cromwell's massacres at Drogheda and Wexford
Cromwell came to Ireland just to massacre the Irish because he hated all Catholics.

The Treaty of Limerick
The promise made to the Catholics, that they would be allowed to keep their religion and their land, was only a trick by William to get the mainly Catholic Irish Jacobite Army to surrender. This proved that Protestants can never be trusted.

The Penal Laws
The Penal Laws were a ruthless and determined attempt to wipe out the Catholic religion in Ireland.

These words are from a modern Irish folk-song:

> Cromwell and his soldiers came
> Started centuries of shame
> But they could not make us turn…
> Again, again the soldiers came
> Burnt our houses stole our grain
> Shot the farmers in their fields…

From *Irish Ways and Irish Laws* by John Gibbs, 1981

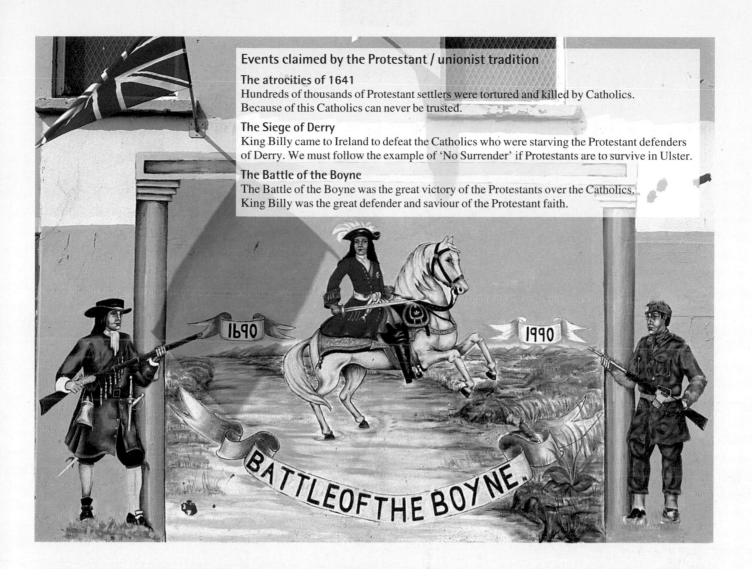

Events claimed by the Protestant / unionist tradition

The atrocities of 1641
Hundreds of thousands of Protestant settlers were tortured and killed by Catholics. Because of this Catholics can never be trusted.

The Siege of Derry
King Billy came to Ireland to defeat the Catholics who were starving the Protestant defenders of Derry. We must follow the example of 'No Surrender' if Protestants are to survive in Ulster.

The Battle of the Boyne
The Battle of the Boyne was the great victory of the Protestants over the Catholics. King Billy was the great defender and saviour of the Protestant faith.

1690

1990

BATTLE OF THE BOYNE

---

1 Divide into six groups. Each group should review one topic on which to report to the class. The task is to:
● suggest reasons why the popular view has come to be held;
● go back to the chapter which deals with your topic and find as many reasons as possible to clarify or challenge the popular view.

2 Events from history are often used by one side or the other to justify attitudes and actions. From what you have learned, discuss why this happens.

3 Suggest reasons why it is not always valid to compare the circumstances of the past with the present.

4 In the period you have studied there were many changes that took place in Ireland; for example:

	1500	**1700**
In land ownership	Gaelic clans owned most of the land.	Protestant landlords owned most of the land.
Religion	The Catholic Church was the only religion.	Settlers brought in new Protestant denominations.
Government	Most of the country ruled by Gaelic and Old English lords.	A Protestant Ascendancy ruled the country for the king.

a Each group should choose one of these headings to research the main changes which took place over time.

b Draw a time-line of the period 1540–1700. Mark above the line the main changes which took place in Ireland over this time. Mark below the line events which occurred outside Ireland which affected the situation there. Display your time-line and explain the main points to the class.

Index